P9-BIG-627

Contents

The Parable of the Mothers and Daughters

Florence Rush[1]

Many years ago when the world was new, there were rivers, trees, plants, birds, animals and people. The people looked very much alike except for some small differences which no one noticed and sometimes some bore and gave birth to little people. They all lived together, hunted and gathered food, played in the water, among the plants, with each other and each other's bodies and all the big people took care of the little ones. When more food was hunted and gathered than was needed for each day, the people used the extra time differently. One who liked music would sing or make sounds with sticks, shells and water while another made pictures in the sand or images of birds on a smooth rock. Even a little person had preferences and if she (everyone was "she" in those days) also loved music and chose to be with the music lover, the big music lover then cared for the little one. So people had different preferences and choices; each could decide what to do with her time and whom to spend it with; each had control and power over her own life and that was very good.

Later when many little people were born, it became difficult to hunt and gather and care for them so all the little ones were cared for in one place. This work was equally shared but soon someone suggested that those with breasts were better able to feed the little ones and should take on the entire job. The breast-people welcomed this change; free from hunting and gathering, they could look around at their world for a better way to live. Soon some planted seeds and grew food, others trained animals to carry heavy loads, animal fur was made into cloth; they built houses, wove baskets, made tools and before long became artists and inventors. Every day the breast-people became smarter and enjoyed a happy, interesting and exciting life.

One day the breastless ones noticed that the breast-people were

4

getting strong and skillfull and growing so much food that hunting and gathering was no longer necessary; furthermore the separation made it obvious that the breast-people bore and gave birth to the little ones. The breast-people happily shared everything with everyone and would have been delighted to have the breastless ones bear and give birth but this could not be shared and this was the only natural difference between them. This difference and the progress of the breast-people, so startled and frightened the breastless ones that they pondered for a way to overcome this fear. So the breastless ones contrived to have control over those they feared and they committed the first crime—they took possession of the lives of the breast-people and their little ones, robbed them of all they created and produced, took away their freedom and made them slaves. Their crime was known as "marriage" and from then on the breastless ones were males and the breast-people, females. With no excuse for this behavior, the males invented a lie to justify their crime; males are superior to females, they said. The females hated captivity, fought, ran away and even killed the males so the males invented more lies; females are weak and need male protection, they said. When resistance continued, the males wrote their lies in books and these books were the Bible, the Koran and the Texts of Hinduism. To be assured of power, what was written became law and those who broke the law were punished so the right of males to enslave females became legal and from then on the males were men and the females, women.

Soon all the women were married; they no longer tried to run away and some even believed what was written. Often several women were married to one man and together they harvested the food, washed clothing in the river and cared for the children. Since the wives did not enslave each other, they were happy together. When the men saw this happiness they remembered when the women were strong and again were frightened and this time they wrote in their books that women must hate, fight and betray each other for the favor of men. So women were made to believe that love between them was not possible and now they had neither power nor love.

Later these books became the foundation of civilizations and the women were made proud to deliver a male child and disgraced by a female child. It was the mother's duty to raise her son to feel superior and her daughter to feel inferior and this was called "socialization." At the risk of punishment or disgrace, the mothers were compelled to train their daughters as slaves and they could not permit them to be inventive or artistic but taught them to carry heavy burdens, submit to the sexual lust of men and bear and rear children. When the daughters were young and their spirit strong, they fought their mothers and ran away but the fathers would catch them and send them back to their mothers to be socialized. But the mothers and daughters knew that each was forced into slavery and when not struggling, they were friends. The mothers protected their daughters as best they could from rape and abuse, fed and clothed them and the daughters danced and gave their mothers flowers and their friendship was their only pleasure and strength. Again jealous, the men demeaned the love of the mothers and daughters; they described it as a strange female compulsion and called it "devotion" and "sacrifice." If women were not devoted or self-sacrificing, the men said they would suffer from a malady called "guilt." So with the threat of guilt, love of the mothers and daughters became a burden and now the men controlled not only the lives of women but their feelings as well. There was no more pleasure for the mothers and daughters. At times they complained but were told that if they suffered in silence they would be rewarded in heaven. Soon the women rarely struggled and because they quietly endured, some men thought the women enjoyed this condition so they called them "lovers of pain" or "masochists."

The men were now truly different from the women. They never knew the joy of love or the pain of guilt; their pleasure was only in power and their sorrow only from the loss of it. Power made them feel so good and strong that fathers and sons began to battle each other and the winner took his prize of land, cattle, women and other men. The lives of the women were unbearably empty so sometimes they fought each other hoping to gain some pleasure from power as the men, but the women had nothing to win from each other—neither land nor wealth; they did not even own their own lives. Men never interfered when women fought because it comforted them to see women divided. When it suited the men they were friendly to one another but when they wanted power they fought and when they fought they killed and when they killed they were rewarded with more wealth and power and although one man lost, another gained, and even the poorest and lowliest man alive had power over some woman. The power of men grew and soon institutions evolved to support them and the church, family and schools established the inferiority of women as truth and the oppression of women as just.[2]

Soon the people no longer lived off the land but from what was produced by machines. They followed the machines to the cities and families were reduced from many wives and relatives to a husband, wife and children. No longer bound to the land, people thought of freedom and wealth and some men became very rich but now the lone woman in the family did the family work and also worked on the machines. There was talk of liberty and democracy and some women listened, thought of their own freedom and just, as their hopes were raised a little, a physician appeared and told the world that women were biologically inferior and masochistic and naturally meant for slavery. Fathers and sons fought for the mother, he said, but the son soon learned that the mother was not worth the struggle, so he allied himself with the powerful father. The daughter also turned to her father, but since she could never be a man, she could only despise the mother who deprived her of a penis, marry, have a baby instead of a penis and accept her inferiority and slavery. So the superior fathers and sons either got along or understandably competed for masculine power while the inferior mothers and daughters hated themselves and each other and were forever afflicted by their female deficiencies. This was written in books and believed by all even the mothers and daughters.

Men became very greedy; they made terrible wars, built bigger machines and began to foul and destroy the earth. The hierarchies of power were getting out of hand, the institutions were crumbling and since women's inferiority was firmly established it was easy to blame them for this devastation. Men plundered and destroyed but when children sickened themselves with drugs and the streets were made unsafe by rapes, mugging and killing, and children ran from home and people were sick from a life without purpose, a group of wise men called psychologists, found the source of disturbance in women, particularly mothers. Then there were some women who, filled with anger by the injustices of the world, fought to free men from war and racial injustice, but no matter how hard they struggled for the freedom of men, the men made speeches while the women were sent to the kitchen and the women knew they were despised. Aware that they gained nothing from the struggle to free men, they formed a movement in their own cause. The women began to talk and trust each other and they discovered that they were strong, even stronger than men; that they were smart, even smarter than men; that they had great capacity for feeling whereas men confused sex urges with emotions. Women wanted control over their lives but the men with power resisted; they fought, ridiculed and humiliated the women, called them man and child-haters, dykes, destroyers of the family and motherhood and spread their venom by their instruments of communication. How to obtain power became a prime problem but it was soon clear that women, so long separated and divided by men according to male class, money, status and education, came to the movement with a variety of backgrounds and experiences and this variety led to differences of opinion. Some claimed that the institutions of oppression must be internally changed and others said they must be attacked from without; some felt all relationships with men must be discontinued and others thought one must live with men to challenge and undermine their power; some turned from marriage and motherhood while others wanted to raise children; many claimed that lesbianism was the real commitment to feminist revolution while others wanted to hide their sexual preference and not offend those who fear the love of women for each other; some advocated socialism, others anarchism, etc. The women did not agree, so with the weight of the centuries of patriarchal power upon them, they began to quarrel and they said one to the other "you are my oppressor." But the technique to keep women apart is told in all the books written by men and in the Parable of the Mothers and Daughters.

Long ago the mothers were forced to press their daughters into slavery but in recent days the practice continues for fear of social scorn or of exclusion. And although the rebellious daughter is no longer captured, she is infused with the lies of her inferiority and stripped of all confidence so that force is no longer needed to prevent her independence.[3] So a woman of twenty-two, unsure of her strength yet wanting freedom, is immobilized. And a woman of fifty or sixty still blames her mother for the bitterness and frustration of her life and this very same woman agonizes over the antagonism between herself and her daughter. But were the mothers to eschew their mother role and the daughters their daughter role both could see that it is the world of men which contrives to mold all women into slaves; that the institutions and machinery of communication can more thoroughly control the daughters than any mother. The desire of the daughter to be slender and attractive will be instilled whether mothers train their daughters to this end or not and since the daughters are doomed never to be slender or attractive enough, so are the mothers doomed to be forever blamed. So in this conflict, devoid of any gratification or victory, the mothers and daughters are trapped. But if the mothers and daughters could walk away, stop blaming each other and loosen the bonds which over the ages have become less visible but no less restrictive, then surely both could see that neither have power nor control over each other but the power which deprives them of freedom, stems from men.

The Parable of the Mothers and Daughters is our story and our conflict. Our struggle with each other betrays our submission to the rule of men. We have no way to control each others' lives or behavior, yet with an illusion of power we also quarrel without gratification or victory. And do we really know what is right or wrong, good or bad for each other; do we have our own ethics, standards and ideology or are we floundering to be feminists within a framework of male definition? What is this power we seek when the only power we know is described by patriarchs and let us think what power can be in feminist terms. What would power mean in a world free of force and coercion; love without a trace of devotion, sacrifice and guilt; sex uncorrupted by power, fear and manipulation? We have much to discover and it may be that our difference will be our strength and the effort to protect each woman's right to be different our greatest unifying force, and this right can be for us all—lesbians, celibates, bisexual, asexual, amazon virgins and heterosexual; for housewives, mothers, laborers, engineers, doctors, plumbers, artists, women of all ages, races, from all places whoever, whatever they are or want to be.

The mothers and daughters have suffered enough at each others' hands as have all women. So if the mothers and daughters do not agree, let them not agree but let them leave each other to find her own way. And if women do not agree, let them not agree and if they must, let them also leave each other. And the strength of women will be each of us and from our variety will come our feminist thinking and all the old ways will be challenged and all the old concepts will be redefined and from our difference, variety, and feminism will come our strength and with this strength we will battle our only oppressor—men![4]

---

1. Jan Peterson and I discussed and agreed upon all the ideas and concepts presented in this paper.

2. See *An Encyclopedia of Religion* ed. Vergilius Ferm, (Littlefield, Adams and Co. New Jersey) 1959 p. 829 "Traditional attitudes towards women in our society are derived largely from the early Christian teachings of the Church Fathers. It was the Apostle Paul who expressed the earliest authoritative opinion of Christianity in regard to the status of women. Women he thought inferior . . . Women were all tainted with the sin of Eve . . . Woman was dangerous to man . . .
Thus the view of woman as a thing both inferior and evil found expression very early in the history of the church."

3. See Eva Figus, *Patriarchal Attitudes* (Fawcett Pub. Inc. Conn) 1970 p. 37 "If one looks at our own civilization one can see a gradual shift from direct physical control to a system of complex and subtle taboos. The shift from external to internal controls one sees between old Jewish and later Christian morality . . . Killing a woman taken in adultery represents direct physical control, but Christ's prohibition against committing adultery in your heart is a form of taboo . . . In the Middle Ages it was still acceptable to beat one's wife or daughter, but by the 19th century there was an effective network of moral taboos which controlled the wives and daughters of the upper and middle class (enforced of course by underlying realities of economic dependence and social ostracism for those who strayed).

4. This is a story and nothing more. Some general references are made to actual people and events but there is no attempt to present anything written here as anthropological or historical fact.

Lesbianism and Feminism

Ti-Grace Atkinson

Since the beginning of this current Movement, feminist activity has been labeled lesbianism. The first time I was called a lesbian was on my first picket line, in front of the New York Times, to desegregate the help-wanted ads. Generally speaking, the Movement has reacted defensively to the charge of lesbianism: 'no, I'm not;' 'yes, you are,' 'no, I'm not;' 'prove it.' For myself, I was so puzzled by the connection that I became curious. Whenever the enemy keeps lobbing bombs into some area you consider unrelated to your defense, it's worth investigating. The Oppressor never has 'mechanical failures'— only the Oppressed does, and then only at strategic and convenient moments.

Why is lesbianism significant for feminism? Since the beginning of this Movement, lesbianism has been a kind of code word for female resistance. Lesbianism is in some way symbolic of feminism as a political movement. While the charge of lesbianism has generally been made by anti-feminists, that fact does not disqualify the relevancy of lesbianism to feminism. The paranoia of one's enemy is frequently both educative and inspirational.

Lesbianism for feminism is not just 'another' issue or 'another' example of human oppression. Nor is lesbianism about 'autonomy.' Lesbianism is pretty clearly about 'association'—not about aloneness. If lesbianism were about aloneness, it could hardly be relevant to anything in a political sense. 'Political' concepts by definition are about society. These concepts must concern at least two or more persons in relationship to one another.

It is the association by choice of individual members of any Oppressed group, the massing of power, which is essential to resistance. It is the commitment of individuals to common goals, and

11

to death if necessary, that determines the strength of an army. In war, even political warfare, there is no distinction between the political and the personal. (Can you imagine a Frenchman serving in the French army from 9 to 5, then trotting 'home' to Germany for supper and overnight? That's called game-playing, or collaboration, not political commitment.)

It is this commitment, by choice, full-time of one woman to others of her class that is called lesbianism. It is this full commitment, against any and all personal considerations if necessary, that constitutes the political significance of lesbianism.

There are women in the Movement who engage in sexual relations with other women, but who are married to men; these women are not lesbians in the political sense. These women claim the right to private lives; they are collaborators.

There are other women who have never had sexual relations with other women, but who have made and live a total commitment to this Movement; these women are lesbians in the political sense.

Lesbianism contains the key principle to a successful feminist revolution: 'guilt' by association. This mark of resistance divides the feminists from the anti-feminists, whether within or outside the Movement. The political essence of lesbianism as synonymous with feminism is being suppressed.

The crucial features of lesbianism are the political and tactical significance of lesbianism to feminism. This involves both analysis and strategy.

Oppression as a phenomenon includes two parties, or classes, the Oppressor and the Oppressed. These parties are artificially created into systems by dichotomizing the human race sequentially on the basis of various pretexts: sex, race, religion, etc. Any given class system, or the phenomenon of oppression, is stabilized by institutions (all of which are by definition 'political'): in the case of women—marriage, motherhood, prostitution, rape, pornography.

But no system is absolutely perfect. There is always at least a tiny minority within the Oppressed who simply *will* not (later co-opted by the Oppressor as *can* not) play out its proper political function in society. This minority is labeled by those in power, the Oppressor, as the 'criminal' element.

The 'criminal' element, when contained—that is, not politicized—serves several functions for the Oppressor. This element is permitted to exist by being bought off by the Oppressor and paid out of the pocket of the Oppressed—crime does pay. But the Oppressor keeps check enough so that there is always sufficient risk (deterrent) to discourage too large a number of the Oppressed from becoming 'criminal.' (The distinction between criminal and revolutionary is quantitative.) The criminal element is the buffer between the Oppressor and the remainder of the Oppressed: criminality is both a safety valve and an object lesson.

The 'criminal' element is, however, seriously dangerous to the Oppressor in only one instance. It is the source of revolutionary leadership. If the Oppressed class begins to get restless, this buffer zone must be removed—annihilated. This removes both the potential leadership for a revolt and serves as a scapegoat or sacrifice to co-opt the rage of the Oppressed. The 'criminal' element is presented by all the propaganda machines as the primary exploiter of the Oppressed. Since most people who've been shit on for thousands of years tend to stink, the Oppressed will usually accept this explanation and help turn over their own people.

Lesbianism is clearly the buffer between the male and female classes. The 'benefits' are primarily a relative degree of independence from the institutional alternatives: marriage, motherhood, prostitution.

The strategic importance of lesbianism to feminism can probably best be understood by analogy, since it is still extremely difficult for people to understand feminism per se in political terms.

The trade union movement originated as a response to desperate working conditions. As this movement grew, an understanding of the *causes* of these conditions evolved. The principle goal of this movement became a reduction of the discrepancy between the incomes of the economic classes.

Numerous and varied socialist theories developed. But the government made a primary distinction between socialist theory, with its relatively un-coordinated actions, and the Communist Party. The Party was 'political' in the sense of directly and publicly attacking the class structure. It was 'militant' socialism.

The witch hunt that followed, on the Communist Party ostensibly, was government terrorism aimed at the socialist principle. And the witch hunt worked. Many people's lives were destroyed by this; many more people fled from socialist thinking. And there was a metamorphosis within the trade union movement.

Our government now has the nerve to talk about labor racketeering. The labor bosses are just small-time entrepeneurs. The government destroyed the principle of unionism, then permits a 'criminal' element to run the government's capitalist show, and *then* proceeds to keep checks on the 'criminals' by timely exposés. Criminality is a relative thing at this time and especially in this country, and our government is in the most embarrassing position to be making accusations.

Lesbianism is to feminism what the Communist Party was to the trade union movement. Tactically, any feminist should fight to the death for lesbianism because of its strategic importance. If the government witch hunts lesbianism (and all feminists have always been aware of this possibility), and if the government *succeeds* in isolating lesbianism to *any* degree from feminism, feminism is lost. Feminism, like unionism, will be a complete racket: feminism will be co-opted and subsumed by its Oppressor.

The Sexual Abuse of Children:
A Feminist Point of View

Florence Rush

When I was asked to talk on the sexual abuse of children, I was not certain where the subject would lead. I am a social worker, had worked for the Society for the Prevention of Cruelty to Children, and remembered that the sexual victims brought to my attention were always female children and that the offenders were always male adults. This triggered off other recollections. I had worked some years back in an institution for dependent and neglected girls. I dug up some old notes and discovered that all those in my caseload had been sexually victimized at one time or another running the gamut from exposure to male exhibitionists, to touching and fondling, to rape, incest and carnal abuse. There was not a single girl who did not have an experience to relate. With my memory set in motion, I went back to when I was 20 and worked in an orphanage one summer between school years. I lived in the institution and was in charge of a summer program for the girls between 7 and 15 years of age. Soon after I began on the job, I learned that the male director would regularly take some of the girls to his apartment and sexually molest them. One night I returned to the institution late to find the director in the hall entrance where he began to fondle and kiss me. The next day I reported his behavior plus his other activities to the Board of Directors. I was questioned very carefully and gently asked if I hadn't encouraged him just a teeny bit. I held my ground and the director was fired. Please do not get the wrong impression. I quickly learned that the director was stealing the institution blind but no one could prove this, and I accomodated the Board by offering a perfect solution to their problem. A week later I was dismissed on the pretext that the institution had run out of funds and could no longer pay my

15

salary. As I walked out the door, the new director, a man, entered. Tearfully the orphans and I said goodbye, and it appeared to me that these children and young women were helplessly prepared to face the same abuse which might be heaped upon them by the new director.

I said to myself at that time that these were poor children, who were unprotected and exposed to the evils of poverty. They came from broken homes, were economically disadvantaged and this could not happen to a child in a stable family situation. This line of thinking, however, did not sit right with me and something kept prodding me to remember more. I did remember more, I remembered about myself. I came from a very stable family which was both culturally and economically advantaged. At age 6, my mother sent me alone to the friendly family dentist who did more feeling than drilling. When I told my mother of my experience, she did not believe me. At age 10, I was molested by the father of a boy I secretly loved and I somehow connected my secret love with the father's treatment of me and felt ashamed and guilty. At 13, my uncle, my mother's brother, came to visit from Chicago and wouldn't keep his hands off me. Again I told my mother and she scolded me for making up stories. Repeated lack of success did teach me never to report such incidents again.

At about the same time, I became obsessed with movies. I loved them, went every time I could, but found I could never get through a double feature without finding the hand of some gentleman up my skirt. My girl friend Jane and I worked out a system. If a man would get "funny", that is if in the middle of a great Fred Astaire and Ginger Rodgers movie, one of us discovered a strange hand between our legs, it was time to get up and say in a loud voice, "I must go home now because my mother is expecting me." Jane and I would then change seats and hope we would be left alone long enough to see the end of the film. It never occurred to us to holler at the man, hit him, or even report him to the management. It never occurred to us to hold the man responsible for what he had done. This was our problem, not his, and we handled it as best we could. In subsequent years, Jane and I reported regularly to each other on the number of exposed men we had seen, how we handled attempts to be touched and how we escaped from what might develop into something violent and dangerous. After a while we became rather casual about our

16

experiences, rarely became outraged, but simply tried to develop greater skills in avoiding and extricating ourselves from the sexual aggression of men without embarrassing the offender. This was excellent training and prepared me in later years for the breast grabbers, the bottom pinchers and the body rubbers. The horror, the shame and the humiliation never left me, but until recently I never knew I had the right to be outraged and fight back. I was, after all, trained to be a woman.

After these memories, my thesis for this presentation became clear. *The sexual abuse of children is an early manifestation of male power and oppression of the female.* For myself, I need no statistics or research to prove my point, but to make my presentation credible, I have searched for supportive evidence. There is, significantly, very little material on the subject of sexual abuse generally and particularly as it relates to children. I think I found enough, however, for my purposes today. I will refer to five studies. The first is the one I have chosen as my authority and is the one most sympathetic to child victims of sex crimes. It is entitled "Protecting the Child Victim of Sex Crimes Committed by Adults" and it is put out by the American Humane Association. I found this report to be the least prejudiced, the most scholarly, most humane and most informative as compared to the other studies I referred to. The following statistics, statements and conclusions are drawn from this study which is based on the investigation of 263 child victims of sexual abuse.

1. National statistics on the incidence of sexual offenses against children are wholly unavailable. The FBI's annual Information Crime Report is concerned with statistics on the offender and not the victim. It does not even carry a breakdown of the total incidence of all crimes against children. What makes an assessment even more difficult, except for rare cases of brutal attack or fatal situations, is that cases of sex offenses against children are not generally publicized by the press.[1]

2. The problem of sexual abuse of children is of unknown national dimensions but findings strongly point to the probability of an enormous national incidence many times larger than the reported

17

incidence of child abuse (physical abuse other than sexual).

3. By an overwhelming ratio, 97%, offenders were male and ranged in age from 17 to 68.

4. Victims were on a ratio of 10 girls to one boy. The victims ranged in age from infants to under 16 and the median age was 11.

5. In 75% of the cases, the offender was known to the child or family such as a father, stepfather, mother's lover, brother, uncle or friend of the family—25% of the offenders were alleged to be strangers.

6. Sixty percent of the child victims were coerced by direct force, or threat of bodily harm. In 25% the lure was based on the child's loyalty and affection for a friend or relative. Fifteen percent were based on tangible lures.

7. Children were subjected to sexual offenses of all types varying from indecent exposure to full intercourse, rape and incest. The majority of incest is between fathers and young daughters.

8. Two thirds of the child victims were found to be emotionally damaged by the occurence with 14% severely disturbed. Twenty-nine of the victims became pregnant as a result of the offense.

9. In 41% of the cases, the offenses were repeated and perpetuated over a period of time ranging from weeks to 7 years.

10. All the cases in the study were reported to the police (263). They made 173 arrests and 106 were released on bail; this resulted in bringing the offender back into the community thus again exposing the child victim to danger.

11. More than 1,000 court appearances were required for the 173 cases prosecuted and this resulted in extreme tension and stress for both child and family. Forty-four percent of the cases were dismissed for lack of proof.

12. In almost 2/3 of the homes, the parents were found to be inadequate. They were deemed to be failing to provide the care and protection necessary for their children's welfare. (I will come back to this last point later).[2]

I will comment now on four other studies. The following quotations and my comments will focus on general and professional attitudes which relentlessly forgives the adult male offender and indicates little concern for the female child victim.* I will refer to the studies as Study Number 1, 2, 3, and 4. I will identify my source material later to anyone who wishes the information.

Study Number 1

This was an investigation of 1,365 convicted male sex offenders—868 offenders committed offenses against children. The following are direct quotes taken from the study.

Not only do they (women) commit fewer illegal sexual acts . . . . but society tends to ignore or tolerate their breaches. Persons hesitate to sign a complaint against a female, police loathe to arrest and juries loathe to convict.

The indifference is justifiable. The average female has a much lower "sex drive" than the average male, consequently she is least likely to behave in a sexually illegal manner.

If a woman, walking past an apartment, stops to watch a man undressing . . . , the man is arrested as an exhibitionist.[3]

I thought I would first like to establish the author's attitude toward women. The author feels that the biologically limited woman with her low sex drives is not driven to commit sex crimes. If she were however, society would be loathe to punish her. On the other hand men, biologically endowed with powerful sex drives, naturally commit sex crimes. Despite his natural propensity toward sex crimes, men are accused of sex crimes which they do not commit. It may be confused, but the author's feelings come through loud and clear. His opinion of women is no secret. Now let us hear what he has to say about children.

The horror with which society views the adult who has sexual relations with young children is lessened when one examines the behavior of other mammals. Sexual activity between adult and immature animals is common and appears to be biologically normal.[4]

Disregard for age, sex and species need not be regarded as biologically pathological; it is precisely what we see in various animals, particularly in certain monkeys.[5]

I once saw my cat have kittens. After each kitten was born, the mother ate the afterbirth and cleaned her babies with her tongue. I've had three children and am delighted I did not have to follow the example of the mother cat. Maybe monkeys are more like us. I don't know, but it never occurred to me that the behavior of animals was the norm for human behavior. The author now explains one kind of sexual offender.

> Exhibitionism is an expression of hostility and sadism; a way to frighten and shock. Very few of these people (exhibitionists) consciously feel hostility and on the whole are to be pitied rather than to be feared.[6]

I guess dirty old men need love too. Again the author's logic eludes me but the contradiciton and bias are obvious.

Study Number 2

Here we have an examination of 41 children and the study attempts to estimate the psychologically harmful affects of sexual assault on children. The author draws heavily on Freudian theories of infant sexuality.

> He (Freud) noted that the majority of children could escape from the sexual situation if they wished and he maintained that the silence shown by some children following seduction, could be explained in terms of their own feeling of guilt in yielding to forbidden attraction . . .

> The girl will strive to counter-act her fear of the bad or sadistic penis by introducing a good one in coitus . . . [7]

> Bender and Blau (experts in child study) noted that the most striking feature of sexually assaulted children was their unusually attractive personalities. This was so noticeable that the authors frequently considered the possibility that the child might have been the actual seducer rather than the one innocently seduced.[8]

> The myth of childhood innocence seems, in the main, to have been rejected and some degree of participation by the victim group is accepted by all studies.[9]

> The suggestion is, therefore, made that the sexual assault of children by adults does not have a particularly detrimental affect on the child's subsequent development . . . The need for affection, which may have well predisposed the child to this form of sexual acting out, will be outgrown.[10]

Isn't it strange how victims are held responsible for offenses against them! Our sexuality as women and children is not used to understand us but to psychologically trap us so that, we are told, the woman seeks to be raped and the little girl wants sexual abuse. And while the woman invites rape and the child invites sexual abuse, men are permitted their sexual indulgences, American soldiers rape and kill Vietnamese women and children and the Hell's Angels roam free to raid and rape. The myth of consent, that is the psychiatric and popular use of ill-defined sexual motivation and acting out to explain and condone the victimization of women and children, is unforgiveable and shameful.

Study Number 3

This study involved a general investigation into the sexual behavior of women. Over 4,000 women were studied and 24% of these reported pre-adolescent experiences with an adult male.

> It is difficult to understand why a child, except for its cultural conditioning, should be disturbed by having its genitalia touched, or disturbed by seeing the genitalia of another person . . . Some of the more experienced students of juvenile problems have come to believe that the emotional reactions of the parents, police and other adults . . . may disturb the child more seriously than the contacts themselves. The current hysteria over sex offenders may well have serious affects on the ability of many children to work out sexual adjustment some years later.[11]

With the usual male arrogance, the author cannot imagine that a sexual assault on a child constitutes a gross and devastating shock and insult, so he blames everyone but the offender. The fact is that sexual offenses are barely noticed except in the most violent and sensational instances. Most sex offenses are never revealed; when revealed, most are either ignored or not reported; if reported a large percentage are dismissed for lack of proof and when proof is established, many are dropped because of the pressure and humiliation forced on the victim and family by the authorities.

Study Number 4

This study deals with 20 cases of incest and involves the fathers as offenders and daughters as victims. The preponderance of incest cases are between fathers and young daughters. The author, although sympathetic with the victim, still does not deal with the offender, but looks to the mother to control the problem.

> There follows several examples of father behavior described by 13 mothers and, in every instance, corroborated by the child victim;

breaking a radio over the mother's head; burning the child with hot irons, chasing the mother out of the house with a gun; . . . locking mother or children in closets while he sexually abused the child victim . . . forcing sexual intercourse with the child in the mother's presence . . . etc.[12]

After examining the character of the incest family . . . the unavoidable conclusion seems to be that the failure of the mother to protect the child against the contingency of incestuous victimization is a crucial and fruitful area of study . . .[13]

Considering the father offender as a possible source of control of incest behavior seems . . . like considering the fox . . . as guard in the henhouse . . .[14]

The mother is the only possible agent of incest control within the family group.[15]

The father rapes and brutalizes and it turns out to be the mother's fault and responsibility. Has anyone thought of the fantastic notion of getting rid of the father? Let me read you a statement of a 14 year old girl taken down by the police.

I was about 9 years old when my father first began to come to my bedroom, which I shared with my two sisters, at night and started to touch my breasts and private parts. This would usually happen in the evening when my mother went to the movies or when she was in the living room and my older sister, Anne, was looking at TV or taking a shower. It was within the same year that my father began to have intercourse with me which is putting his penis into my private parts. This was very painful to me when it started. My father told me this was normal and all girls did this with their fathers. When I said I was going to tell my mother or someone about it, he said that what my mother does not know would not hurt her. Sometimes he would hit me when I would refuse him and at times he would take me in the car and, as we rode, touch my vagina.[16]

This completes my report on the studies. I would like to touch very briefly on the subject of female juvenile delinquency. Although female juveniles have a much lower crime rate than male juveniles, the female is reported to be involved in a larger percentage of sexual offenses such as sexual promiscuity, adolescent pregnancy and prostitution. Although these offenses are all heterosexual and cannot be indulged without the male, the male is rarely regarded as the offender. When a girl rebels against her family or society, she is usually suspected by her family and the community of being sexually

22

promiscuous and is thought of as either a slut or a whore. The young male offender, however, is associated with crimes against society, property, etc. Here is a statement from a psychoanalytic journal regarding male and female juvenile delinquency, which supports psychiatrically the popular attitudes towards male and female delinquency.

> The boy's typical delinquent activities contain elements of keen interest in reality; we recognize his fascination with the struggle waged between himself and people, social institutions and the world of nature. In contrast to this, the adolescent girl . . . will . . . take revenge on her mother, by whom she feels rejected, by seeking sexual relations . . .

> In female delinquency, the infantile instinctual organization . . . finds bodily outlet in genital activity. The pregenital instinctual aims . . . relate her delinquency to perversion. An adolescent boy, . . . caught in an ambivalent conflict with his father, might defend himself . . . by getting drunk, destroying property, or stealing a car. . . . His actions are . . . an attempt at progressive development.[17]

If we get past the psychiatric mumbo jumbo, we are told that delinquent boys are trying to grow and develop, while delinquent girls take revenge on their mothers and are trapped in perversion by their "pregenital instinctual aims."

Earlier, I referred to a statistic which noted that 2/3 of the families of sexually abused children were inadequate. According to most anthropologists and sociologists, the purpose of the family is the protection of children. From what I have heard, read and seen, it would seem to me that the protectors and the offenders are one and the same. The fact is that families, generally, are given the job of socializing children to fill prescribed roles and thus supply the needs of a power society. My mother's inability to protect me from sexual abuse did not occur because she was worse than any other mother, but because, like all women, she was guilty and repulsed by her own sexuality and taught me to feel the same way. Seventy-five percent of the sexually abused children are victims of family members or friends. All children suffer at the hands of their family whether the abuse be sexual, physical, or emotional, but children have nowhere to go outside the family. They have no options, no choices and no power. Ingrained in our present family system is the nucleus of male power and domination and no matter how often we witness the devastatingly

23

harmful affects of this arrangement on women and children, the victims are asked to uphold the family and submit to its abuse. Let me read to you from a publication called "Violence Against Children." The passage is part of a study on the physical abuse against children in the United States, completed at Brandeis University; Advanced Studies in Social Welfare.

> Most societies, including America . . . have not developed absolute cultural and legal sanctions against the use of physical force towards children by adults. Not only is such use of physical force not prohibited, but it is even encouraged by many societies . . .

> Children were considered property of their parents in many societies and parents had, thus, absolute power over life and death.[18]

> Children in America . . . have always been subjected to a wide range of physical and non-physical abuse by parents and other caretakers . . . and indirectly by society as a whole. Such abusive treatment of children seems to be inherent in the basic inequality of physical make up and social status between adults and children, and . . . permissive or even encouraging attitudes toward the use of physical force.[19]

It is assumed that because children are not fully grown, they have not the knowledge, the humanity, nor the feeling to know what they want. As women we are treated the same way and children feel as we do, only more so, because they are even more helpless and dependent. It is interesting to note, however, how early and eagerly, male children take on and integrate the attitudes and advantages of male supremacy. I talked one evening to a group of high school students, young men and women about 14 years of age. When I pointed to the similarities between the oppression of women and children, the male students objected vehemently almost to the point of physical revulsion. Already contaminated, they could not bear to be identified with women. But for those male children who are not yet contaminated and for all the female children who are being abused, manipulated, and prepared for the role of subjugation and exploitation, we must offer help in light of our own oppression and new feminist understanding. We must begin to study and understand what is happening to children today.

From my personal experience as a woman, as a female child, as a social worker and, after talking to countless women, after reading and researching, and with my deepened understanding and radicalization from my involvement in the women's movement, I have drawn some conclusions regarding the sexual abuse of children.

1. That the sexual abuse of children, who are overwhelmingly female, by sexual offenders, who are overwhelmingly male adults, is part and parcel of the male dominated society which overtly and covertly subjugates women.

2. That the sexual molestation and abuse of female children is not regarded seriously by society, is winked at, rationalized and allowed to continue, through a complex of customs and mores which applauds the male's sexual aggression and denies the female's pain, humiliation and outrage.

3. That sexual abuse of children is permitted because it is an unspoken but prominent factor in socializing and preparing the female to accept a subordinate role; to feel guilty, ashamed, and to tolerate, through fear, the power exercised over her by men.

4. That the female's early sexual experiences prepare her to submit in later life to the adult forms of sexual abuse heaped on her by her boy friend, her lover, and her husband. In short, the sexual abuse of female children is a process of education which prepares them to become the wives and mothers of America.

5. That the family itself is an instrument of sexual and other forms of child abuse, and that in order to protect children, we must find new ways of rearing them so they may have optimum opportunity to achieve full human growth and potential.

6. That we must begin to think of children's liberation as being the same as women's liberation. The female child and woman are the same person, merely at a different stage of development. The growth from childhood to adulthood is a process, not a "gap" or separation. The female infant, child, woman and old woman are subject to the same evils. The separations are false, provoke hostility and are used to divide us.

In closing, let me read a passage from Shulamith Firestone's book, "The Dialectics of Sex."

> Children then, are not freer than adults. They are burdened by a wish fantasy in direct proportion to the restraints of their narrow lives; with an unpleasant sense of their own physical inadequacy and ridiculousness; with constant shame about their dependence, economic and otherwise;

and humiliation concerning their natural ignorance of practical affairs. Children are repressed at every waking minute. Childhood is hell.

Except for the ego rewards in having children of one's own, few men show any interest in children ... So it is up to the feminist revolutionaries to do so. We must include the oppression of children in any program for feminist revolution or we will be subject to the same failing of which we have so often accused men; of not having gone deep enough in our analysis.

There are no children yet able to write their own book or tell their own story. We will have to, one last time, do it for them.[20]

1. Vincent De Francis. *Protecting the Child Victim of Sex Crimes.* (Denver; The American Humane Association, Children's Division, 1965) pamphlet.
2. Vincent De Francis. *Protecting the Child Victim of Sex Crimes Committed by Adults.* (Denver; The American Humane Association, Children's Division, 1966) pp. 1-3, 215-233.
* In many of the quotations words and phrases have been deleted only to clarify and emphasize. The deletions did not alter the essential meaning of the quotations.
3. Paul Gebhart, et. al. *Sex Offenders.* (New York; Harper and Row, 1965) pp. 9,10.
4. Ibid. p. 54
5. Ibid. p. 276
6. Ibid. p. 399
7. Lindy Burton. *Vulnerable Children.* (New York; Schocken Books, 1968) p. 29.
8. Ibid. p. 104
9. Ibid. p. 113
10. Ibid. p. 169
11. Alfred Kinsey, et. al. *Sexual Behavior in the Human Female.* (New York; Pocket Books, 1953) p. 121
12. Yvonne Tormes. *Child Victim of Incest.* (Denver; The American Humane Association, Children's Division) pamphlet, p. 27
13. Ibid. p. 32
14. Ibid. p. 33
15. Ibid. p. 35
16. De Francis, op. cit., p. 112
17. Peter Blos. "Preoedipal Factors in the Etiology of Female Delinquency," *The Psychoanalytic Study of the Child.* (New York; International Universities Press, 1957) Vol. XII, p. 232
18. David Gil. *Violence Against Children.* (Waltham; Harvard University Press, 1970) p. 9
19. Ibid. p. 1
20. Shulamith Firestone. *The Dialectics of Sex.* (New York; William Morrow and Company, 1970) pp. 117, 118.

The New Misandry

Joanna Russ

Gee, isn't it awful for women to hate men?

Of course lots of men despise women, but that's different; woman-hating isn't serious—at worst it's eccentric, at best sort of cute. Woman-haters (many of whom are women) can express themselves all over the place, as the latest cartoon about women drivers reminds me, but man-haters have fewer opportunities. Man-hating takes self-control. Besides, man-haters are in the minority; for every Valerie Solanas, how many rapists, how many male murderers are there? What male reviewer found Hitchcock's "Frenzy" one-20th as revolting as Solanas's "Scum Manifesto?" Of course Solanas went out and did it, but then so do many, many men—in the small town I live in there were several incidents of rape last year, and a common response to them was laughter.

Alas, it's nothing new for the oppressed to be solemnly told that their entry to Heaven depends on not hating the oppressor; labor is supposed not to hate management and black is not supposed to hate white because hatred is bad. It's a fine case of double-think. Watch: (1) You do something nasty to me. (2) I hate you. (3) You find it uncomfortable to be hated. (4) You think how nice it would be if I didn't hate you. (5) You decide I ought not to hate you because hate is bad. (6) Good people don't hate. (7) Because I hate I am a bad person. (8) It is not what you did to me that makes me hate you, it is my own bad nature. *I—not you—am the cause of my hating you.*

For some reason misandry (a fancy word for man-hating) is a very loaded topic. People even talk as if hating men meant murdering all of them right away—as if there were no difference between feelings and acts. Man-haters are people who feel a certain way (not even all the time, believe it or not); they aren't Instant Murderesses. If misandrists

27

were the uncontrolled, ravening wild beasts they are supposed to be, they would've been strangled in their cradles. Surely very few of us are seriously afraid that battalions of ardent feminist misandrists will come marching out of the sunrise to castrate every man between here and California—though the jokes that are told seem to indicate we think so. Does Betty Friedan really think this will happen? Obviously not. Does Jill Johnston? Hardly. Yet Jill Johnston provokes such extraordinarily virulent abuse that she must be hitting a nerve of some sort and Betty Friedan recently accused Gloria Steinem (of all people) of—what? *Hating men*. A serious charge.

Feminists who want feminism to be respectable are afraid the "radicals" will go "too far." That is, man-hating gives the show away—we aren't merely liberals; our complaints are drastic; we're demanding not asking; we're breaking the mold in the most thorough way possible; *we really mean it*. (That is why "Man-hating" is used as a red herring—it's such a loaded charge.) Movement women who come down hard in public on misandry are afraid of male backlash. They want men's (and women's) cooperation, they want acceptance, they want popularity.

Second, there are women who feel that their own choice of a life-style (living with a man, sleeping with a man, working with men, loving a man) is somehow inpugned or rendered invalid by women who hate men. The second group, of course, feels exactly the same way about the first group—but *that's* been going on for years. The novelty is that the conventional, socially approved choice is now open to question at all. Americans seem to be acting this way lately; we don't love ourselves enough to value our choices without some kind of outside sanction. So we deprecate others lest they deprecate us, even by implication.

Perhaps the most important cause of the fear of misandry is the awfulness of facing the extent to which misandry and misogyny are an inescapable part of the texture of our lives. It is all right to joke about "the battle of the sexes" but we must not take it seriously for the paradoxical reason that it is too serious—every man is a misogynist, how can he help it? and every woman is a misandrist, how can she help it? The misandry, of course, is far far worse that the misogyny—thus giving us a clue as to who the aggressor is in the "battle." While every woman is not Valerie Solanas, Solanas is Everywoman—this means that nobody can escape the general situation. True, some employers are nicer than others. But a job is still a job. True, the enemy isn't shooting at Yossarian in particular. But they're still shooting at him.

We are all, to a very large and uncomfortable degree, prisoners of the institutions in which we live. Being forced to endure awful things is bad enough; we are forced to *feel* awful things, too—it is truly horrible to realize how much stunting and deformation has been forced upon us. It's so much easier to say that everything (as Perelman puts it) is leeches and cream, that all women really love men, that only "sick" women hate men. It is even getting so that to say something is the "wrong" thing to do in a practical, tactical sense, carries overtones of moral condemnation. (Hence Friedan's condemnation of Steinem, et al.) If you are to accept there are women who do indeed openly hate men and that they hate men either because they have hit extreme (but characteristic) circumstances or because they are more clear-sighted than the rest of us, that means you must accept misandry as a possibility for all women. If you are a woman, that means you must accept misandry as a possibility *for yourself*. (If you are a man, this acceptance means you must accept the possibility of women's hatred as a rational response to a bad situation and that you must not get aggrieved at it.) To accept misandry is to perceive what dreadful messes are made of our lives even if we are lucky enough to escape the worst effects of our social structure. There are two kinds of women who never hate men: the very lucky and the very blind.

I think we ought to decide that man-hating is not only respectable but honorable. To be a misandrist a woman needs considerable ingenuity, originality, and resilience. A misogynist requires no such resources. Our men are brought up to hate us; it is the unconventional, intelligent, sensitive, truthful, original man who can get out from under that tyranny and love women. We are brought up to love our men—uncritically and in fear of the consequences if we don't. (I am not talking about this or that particular man, but men as a group. The doctrine that men ought to be accepted or rejected as individuals is a life-saver to women who are horrified by man-hating.

But these very women know perfectly well that the issue is a class issue—they themselves argue that "men" are wonderful, that "men" are good, i.e., they almost always accept the class terms of the argument until some other person gets them off the hook by bringing in the individualist argument that people must be judged singly and then sliding imperceptibly into the stand that people do not belong to groups or classes at all.) It is the unconventional, truthful, sensitive, intelligent, original woman who can get out from under *that* tyranny and see clearly that to be discriminated against, patronized, belittled, frustrated, limited, treated without respect, and taught that one is not important are hardly breeding grounds for Love.

It's possible to reject misandry as a tactic, or even choose to suppress it in oneself, and yet to accept the misandrists themselves. This would involve recognizing misandry as a permanent possibility in every woman's situation and therefore in her life. It would mean not being nervous about what men would think of those awful, man-hating women. It would mean criticizing man-haters—if at all—in private.

Women's situation with respect to men isn't just oppressive; it's terribly confusing. As Virginia Woolf says, neither flattery, affection, ease in her company, nor love will prevent a woman from being put in her place. (Bad things happen not only when the subordinate gets uppity but when the superior gets irritable and wants somebody to take it out on—we all admire the delicate realism of the cartoon in which Boss yells at Husband, Husband yells at wife, and wife yells at Child. That Child had better have a Dog.)

That bad things are done to you is bad enough; worse is the double-think that follows. The man insists—often semi-sincerely, though he has some inkling of his motives because if you question them, he gets mad—that (1) he didn't do anything, you must be hallucinating; (2) he did it but it's trivial and therefore you're irrational ("hysterical") to resent it or be hurt; (3) it's important but you're wrong to take it personally because he didn't mean it personally; (4) it's important and personal but you provoked it, i.e., it's your fault and not his. Worse still, he often insists on all of them at once. In this sort of ideologically mystified situation, clarity is crucial. Let us get several things clear: hurting people makes them angry, anger turns to hate when the anger is chronic and accompanied by helplessness, and although you can bully or shame people into not showing their anger, the only way to stop the anger is to stop the hurt. The cure for hate is power—not power to hurt the hurter, but *power to make the hurter stop*.

It is a mistake to think that man-hating is a delicate self-indulgence; it's very unpleasant. Nor is it a pathological rarity; nothing could be more common. Go look at popular art meant for women: romance magazines, "women's" movies, modern Gothics. Where there is no disguised revenge (as there is in the presentation of the stupid, feeble males of the old radio soaps) there is abundant helplessness, pain, and self-hatred. I find hating others morally preferable to hating oneself; it gives the human race a backbone. It is the first of all the biological virtues, self-preservation, and it takes more bravery than you might think. And before you sneer at self-preservation and declare that self-immolation is wonderful (especially for women) remember that self-sacrifice is a virtue *always* forced on oppressed groups. (Some women twist the "virtue" of self-sacrifice and Love into weapons for themselves: i.e., the guilt-making "I sacrificed everything for you" and the more-loving-than-thou crowd, who treat a spontaneous emotion as if it were a cultivated moral characteristic. They are very snotty to women who don't love as much as they do.)

Why is man-hating so dreadful? Because it is easier for everybody, male and female, to demand saintly purity of the oppressed than to tee off on the oppressor. It's about time we stopped worrying about whether feminists are saints: they're not, quite predictably. And it's also time to scotch that perennial silliness about avoiding Change because Change will provoke a Backlash. Change always provokes a backlash. If you meet with no resistance, you're not doing your political job. As Philip Slater says in "The Pursuit of Loneliness," "backlash" is what happens when people find out that change means change. Pious statements that feminism is really very moderate and harmless aren't going to deceive anybody for long. The radicalism of a cause doesn't come from the individual wishes of a few well-known leaders but from the situation in which large, large numbers of people find themselves. Feminism is radical. Those who don't want to be "that" radical are finding themselves either outstripped or ignored;

31

they become (sadly) the darlings of an Establishment which likes them for all the wrong reasons.

To condemn misandry is to have higher standards of conduct for women than for men. It is to be so frightened about feminism per se that not a taint of ordinary human corruption can be allowed into it. It is to accept the idea of oppression only on the condition that the real, ugly effects of oppression be denied. It is to consider feminism a moral movement and not a political movement—men are okay but we've got to be better.

Isn't that what we were trying to get away from in the first place?

Emily Dickinson Feminist

Rebecca Patterson

Young Emily Dickinson, according to Amherst legend, once told her sister she had a horror of death, the dead were so soon forgotten, but she would make people remember her. The story rings true. On the evidence of the poems she did have a horror of death and a most unfeminine desire for fame, and the two fed upon each other. The more desperate the struggle to realize herself, to become an autonomous human being, the thicker grew the cluster of death images in her work. At the onset of her final illness she said the doctor called it a revenge of the nerves, and it is believable that she died exhausted by the tensions of an unachieved life.

This suffering began in early childhood, and she experienced it as an absence of love, but it was more accurately an absence of possibility. Her first memory was a sense of loss, of being a prince cast out of his dominions, a mourner among the other children. She described herself as starving, as dying of thirst and cold, yet forbidden to take a step toward saving herself. The countless petty denials and prohibitions which were the lot of a little girl became a resentful memory that she must not enter the alluring "woods" because a "snake" might bite her or a "goblin" kidnap her. Prison was a frequent metaphor, for she remembered the shades of the prison house closing around her in a more sinister sense than her brother Austin or any other young male would ever know them. In a rare burst of fellow-feeling her niece, Martha Dickinson Bianchi, said she had been "cramped, curbed, repressed in every natural desire or impulse," only to add at once, and correctly, that this was the "universal condition" to which the more stolid girl friends submitted without apparent pain. Her first editor, Mabel Loomis Todd, was inclined to blame the father, and even the brother, for not realizing

33

that "fine intellectual women" needed special treatment—presumably handsomer, more commodious cells than the generality of Victorian women. In a world where money was power Emily was obliged to beg for postage stamps and to thank her father for buying the books which he audibly deplored her reading. At twenty-eight she could still be disciplined by her brother or fetched home in disgrace by her father when he thought she had stayed out too late. Yet the alternatives to such crippling, infantile dependency were hardly more inviting.

It was an age when poor girls did unpaid domestic and farm work or spent fourteen hours a day in the textile mills for a weekly wage of a quarter or fifty cents above the charges of their company boarding houses. At a slightly higher level a few girls taught school, usually for little more than their board and room; and their fathers appropriated their small earnings as of right. Emily's friend Susan Gilbert tried school teaching for a year and decided, without enthusiasm, that marriage was a better way for a poor girl to earn her living. There is no more than a hint that Emily herself ever thought of seeking work outside her father's house. In a poem, "Frigid and sweet Her parting Face," she blames the other woman for refusing to share "Penury" with her; but it is hopeless to ask whether she thought of teaching school like Sue or of living by her pen like Elizabeth Browning's heroine Aurora Leigh or like Mrs. Browning herself. Although a few women were beginning to set up as authors, it would have been a daring dream.

Lydia Maria Child, whose *Letters from New York* Emily read and admired, thought that literature need no longer be "Deemed a disparagement to woman, and even professed authorship does not involve loss of caste in society." In Sue's copy of a two-volume edition of Elizabeth Browning's *Poems* Emily discovered that the editor, H. T. Tuckerman, thought the writing of genuine verse "an excellent safety-valve" for a woman. He had heard "the publication of a lady's effusions regretted by one of her sex, on the ground that she had 'printed her soul,' " and though the objection was "not without significance to a refined nature," he was happy to point out that very few people read poetry and the exposure of soul would be limited to a select audience. Still he was ready to "acknowledge that authorship, as a career, is undesirable for a woman." A Mrs. S.C. Hall, writing about author Jane Porter for *Harper's Magazine*, which Emily faithfully read, could not settle to her subject until she had genuflected to woman's sacred role of watching over, moulding, and inspiring England's sons. Even though an occasional woman like Jane Porter achieved fame without neglecting the womanly sphere, yet it was certain that as Woman she "would have been happier had she continued enshrined in the privacy of domestic love and domestic duty." Josiah Holland, husband of Emily's good friend, developed this idea at length in his exemplary novel *Miss Gilbert's Career*, which came out in late 1860, just as Emily was getting into the swing of her own career. Since she read it as a friend's book and therefore felt it more keenly, it is worth looking at for a moment.

At the outset Fanny Gilbert is distracted by a plethora of glamorous possibilities:

> She would write books. She would reveal her life in poetry, the music of whose numbers would charm the world, and compel the world to give her homage . . . She would become a great painter . . . She would become a visitor of prisons, and a minister of mercy to the abodes of infamy and of misery, and win immortality for a life devoted to works of charity . . . She would stand before public assemblies, and there assert, not only her own womanhood, but the rights of her sex. She would have a career of some kind.

> In one brief hour of dreaming, all the charms of domestic home-life had faded. The thought of marriage, its quiet duties and its subordination of her life and will to the life and will of another, became repulsive to her.

To her father she declares that it is "a curse to be a woman. I never knew a woman who was not a slave or a nonentity, nor a man who did not wish to make her one or the other . . . I say that I will not accept this lot, and that I do not believe my Maker ever intended I should accept it." Dr. Gilbert orders her to stop insulting him and disgracing herself. When Fanny confides to Miss Hammett that she has written a novel, this friend dilates on the terrible thought of "making my name public property—of permitting it to go abroad as an author, subject to criticism, and to unjust and frivolous judgments . . . of coining my heart's best emotions and my sweetest imaginations into words which the world can use as a glass by which it may read my life." Fanny persists in her unwomanliness, however, and by the time she is twenty-seven has become rich and famous and has discovered that it is all vanity and ashes. She now renouces her career, marries the self-educated clergyman Arthur Blague (who seems meagerly equipped to support them), and learns that woman's true calling is to subdue herself to a good man's career.

Potboiler the book may be, but it does reflect the consistent and serious opinions of its author, and Emily could not help being affected, even wounded, by this travesty of her secret ambitions. Her biographer, George F. Whicher, commenting on a poem in which she declared she would rather starve in her garret than publish her "Snow," dismissed the idea that she could believe such gentility nonsense; but it is difficult to live in a persistently rainy climate without experiencing a certain dampness in the soul.

Her first effort to write seemed to Emily only a little less daring than the primal disobedience of Eve. In a letter to a friend the nineteen-year-old girl told her dear Jane that she had "dared to do strange—bold things" and had "heeded beautiful tempters," and though she could not think herself wrong, she imagined Jane would "tremble and be very much afraid, and wonder how things would end." Her life now had an aim and the world had become "almost too precious for [Jane's] poor—and striving sister!" To another girl friend she wrote that she was "dreaming a *golden* dream, with eyes all the while wide open," and it was a dangerously ambitious and unwomanly dream, for she went on to reject the feminine role with a scornful "God keep me from what they call *households*." A few months later she admitted that her friend might be wiser in submitting to the common lot,

> nipping in the bud fancies which I let bloom—perchance to bear no fruit, or if plucked, I may find it bitter. The shore is safer, A., but I love to buffet the sea—I can count the bitter wrecks here in these pleasant waters, and hear the murmuring winds, but oh, I love the danger!

She had picked up this language from Emerson's "Heroism" ("the fair girl who repels interference by a decided and proud choice of influences" is saluted with the words "O friend, never strike sail to a fear! Come into port greatly, or sail with God the seas"), and Emerson in turn had got it from the German feminist Bettina von Arnim

36

("whoever does not free his thoughts and venture out into the vast, shoreless ocean with his mind, will never act and never reach the Deity, because obeying the will of others is not action . . . I spread my sails and dip forward to rend the chains that bar the port, because it is my will to meet God on the open sea"). So exciting and so difficult and, in the end, so impossible it was for a woman in the nineteenth century to become an authentic human being!

Emily's first poetry was nourished in part by her crush attachment to young Susan Gilbert. When her friend decided in 1853 to marry Austin Dickinson, the poetry soon came to a discouraged stop, and Emily was left miserable without quite knowing why. A glum period of some four or five years ended about the time of her twenty-eighth birthday in a series of exciting discoveries. Apparently in late 1858, her sister-in-law introduced her to Elizabeth Browning's *Aurora Leigh*, a verse-novel about a successful woman poet, and this book revived her ambition and helped carry her poetry in a swelling triumph that crested in 1862-1863. Quite early in January 1859 an old school friend of Sue's, the beautiful young widow Kate Scott Turner, began a first visit which lasted two months and was followed by several other visits over the next two years. Since Kate was a lover of poetry and quite ready to fall in love with Emily's, her admiration was another powerful support. Late in January a third important influence arrived with the February *Atlantic Monthly* containing Thomas Wentworth Higginson's attack on entrenched prejudice under the sardonic title "Ought Women to Learn the Alphabet?" The three young women read it together.

Mrs. Bianchi described her aunt as an "instinctive feminist" and said that even in her youth she had been indignant "at being counted as *non compos* in a man's world of reality." She recalled some of her aunt's gibes at the male professors who were beginning to abound in Amherst. "Most such are Manikins," Emily once wrote, little dreaming they would avenge themselves by writing her biography. Without doubt she was aware of the lively feminist movement which had sprung up in her girlhood at the Seneca Falls Convention of 1848 and was now growing strongly under such leaders as Higginson. When the two met in August 1870 she was eager to tell him of her reading in the work of feminist Lydia Maria Child. She even expected him to catch a feminist allusion which he in fact muffed. He reported in a letter that evening, and again long after her death, that she had said of her household tasks, "& people must have puddings," with so special an intonation, "as if they were comets," that he was left wondering at an emphasis as mystifying as it was meaningless. But Higginson should have remembered—it was prominent enough in the literature—that the pudding had become a feminist symbol for the detested menial work of women (with interesting unconscious associations as well).

As early as 1790 the forgotten New England feminist Judith Sargent Murray demanded whether "a candidate for immortality . . . an intelligent being . . . should at present be so degraded, as to be allowed no other ideas, than those which are suggested by the mechanism of a pudding." In 1838 Sarah Grimké took up the theme with scorn for the male dictum that "she that knoweth how to compound a pudding is more desirable than she who skilfully compounds a poem." If this was Emily's source, then her remark was a sly gibe at Higginson who had been notably unimpressed by her poetry. Grimké's book was well known in England and may have inspired a more famous feminist diatribe. "It is in vain to say human beings ought to be satisfied with tranquility," cried Charlotte Bronte's Jane Eyre; ". . . women feel as men feel; they need exercise for their faculties, and a field for their efforts as much as their brothers do; they suffer from too rigid a constraint, too absolute a stagnation, precisely as men would suffer; and it is narrow-minded in their more privileged fellow-creatures to say that they ought to confine themselves to make puddings . . ." As recently as 1929 a writer on women's education, Thomas Woody, outraged the shade of Sarah Grimké with the condescending remark that it was "a rare accomplishment to be able to translate Epictetus, embroider beautifully, and make a pudding!" There was something about puddings that set a feminist's teeth on edge.

"Ought Women to Learn the Alphabet?" was Higginson's most famous, most reprinted essay. He himself appeared bewildered by its success, although he may never have dreamed that it had more to do with Emily's seeking him out in mid-April 1862 than the more immediate incitement of his "Letter to a Young Contributor" in the April *Atlantic Monthly*. She saw him as a man who could sympathize with the ambitions of women. Her sister-in-law was just as impressed, and about mid-February 1862 begged her friend Samuel Bowles, then in New York, to find her a photograph of this notable leader of the women's movement. An angry, dissatisfied woman, scarcely able to tolerate her unfortunate husband, Sue Dickinson sought all her life for something to give her the consequence she found herself missing. One of the conditions of her marriage appeared to be that it should not be consummated, and as late as 1859, when she wrote her *maiden* name into a newly acquired work by feminist Bettina von Arnim,she seemed to be, not giving up her marriage, but confirming the fact that it had never existed. At some time she noticed in her copy of Tennyson's *The Princess* the line "You hold the woman is the better man," and she firmly bracketed the words "the woman is the better man." She also marked with approval Princess Ida's proposal to do away with love:

> Love is it? Would this same mock-love, and this
> Mock-Hymen were laid up like winter bats,
> Till all men grew to rate us at our worth,
> Not vassals to be beat, nor pretty babes
> To be dandled, no, but living wills, and sphered
> Whole in ourselves and owed to none. Enough!

This passage appears to explain the curious fact that on his return from Europe in late 1862 Samuel Bowles sent Emily a "little bat." Whether a child's bat, a picture of a mammalian bat, or a piece of cotton batting remains unsure, but Tennyson's meaning could be disputed also, and probably was disputed during a lively discussion of women's rights in Sue's parlor two years earlier.

In the beginning Bowles was no friend to women's rights, although he was sensitive enough to find something amiss in a world where women were swallowed up and annihilated as human beings. On the birth of a friend's son, he wrote: "I am glad it is a boy. Boys are institutions. They have a future, a positive future. Girls are swallowed up,—they are an appendage,—a necessary appendage, it may be,—probably they are—but still they are appendages."

On August 5, 1860, Bowles was in Amherst to report the Commencement proceedings for the Springfield *Daily Republican*. When he took time out for refreshment at the younger Dickinsons', he probably did not anticipate running into a barrage of women's rights.

Attacked by two such handsome women as Sue Dickinson and Kate Turner, whom he greatly admired, and by so brilliant a woman as Emily Dickinson, who counted for much less, Bowles began to waver. Emily appeared to be the most aggressive, lavishing contempt on the trivial occupations of women. She may have quoted the lines marked in her own copy of *Aurora Leigh* in which Mrs. Browning's heroine is equally contemptuous. Apparently the discussion turned to Higginson's thesis that only women educated "like boys" ever rose to fame, for Bowles appeared afterwards to be perfectly familiar with Emily's boyish claims. He denounced her as "a provoking (a damned) rascal," a mannish Sally Brass out of *The Old Curiosity Shop*, and she called him a Dick Swiveller. Perhaps she now gave him another taste of Higginson: " 'Earth waits for her queen' was a favorite motto of Margaret Fuller's; but it would be more correct to say that the queen has waited for her earth, till it could be smoothed and prepared for her occupancy." Bowles began jokingly to call the sisters-in-law "queens." Sue was the "queen of Pelham," "queen of the tropics," and Emily, with a touch of contempt, the "Queen Recluse." Or perhaps they earned their queenship by quoting Higginson's remark that "the exclusion of women from all direct contact with affairs can be made far more perfect in a republic than is possible in a monarchy, . . . as matters now stand among us, there is no aristocracy but of sex: all men are born patrician, all women are legally plebeian."

Beneath the social manners and the joking tone there may have been some sharpness, for Emily sent a playful but apologetic note after Bowles, asking him to forgive a boyish "little Bob o' Lincoln." Sam Bowles, however, had gone away less angry than thoughtful. He read *Aurora Leigh* and thanked Sue for recommending it to him; he planned to take no other book except the Bible on his trip to Europe. He read Margaret Fuller's *Woman in the Nineteenth Century*, perhaps again on Sue's recommendation, and prepared to deal with Josiah Holland's chauvinistic *Miss Gilbert's Career*. He began his review with care, for though he regarded his former editor as a canting prig, he knew that canting prigs were good for circulation, but he finished with a ringing declaration of support for some "gray-eyed 'woman of the nineteenth century' " affronted by this book. Shortly afterwards he sent the review to his good friend Maria Whitney and told her that she and two or three unnamed women had changed his opinion of their sex.

In condemning herself to perpetual boyhood, Emily may have made the best possible compromise with her times, although it was a serious limitation on the development of her work. As a "boy" in her father's house she could largely control her inner conditions, read as she liked, explore her inner environment, devote an enormous amount of time to her writing. Her father left her pretty much alone, and her mother and sister could have invaded Mars more readily than her mind. Marriage was out of the question. Even if she could have borne the sexual intimacy, which is doubtful, as a wife she would have been destroyed. It was simply that for women in the nineteenth century marriage was so dreadful, as anthropologist Ralph Linton once remarked, that they could be driven into it only by making the alternatives still more dreadful. This was an exceptional woman, highly intelligent, greatly gifted, and the hiding of the one talent would have been as deadly to her as it ever was to John Milton. Yet the whole intent of marriage—and this was freely admitted on all hands—was to destroy talent, to cripple, shame, belittle, reduce women of talent to the same convenient, domestic stereotype. *Miss Gilbert's Career* was poor fiction but an accurate reflection of its age. And of a later age, perhaps?

There is a curious echo in the work of a modern poet. The tragic heroine of Sylvia Plath's *The Bell Jar* rages against the flattening out underfoot like a kitchen mat which her young man demands of her, the "sinister, knowing way" in which he assures her—he is training to be a psychiatrist—that after she has had children she won't want to write poems any more. She begins to see marriage as a kind of brainwashing which numbs a woman into slavery in a "private, totalitarian state." A still more striking example appears in a recent psychiatric study of Emily herself, John Cody's *After Great Pain*. Given adequate "nurturance" by the mother, this doctor believes, Emily could have been made a "contented housewife." The light upon the poet may be of the murkiest, but it absolutely blazes on a bundle of archaic demands and prejudices persisting deep into the twentieth century. The poetry for which this woman gave her life is of less importance than a kitchen mop.

41

It is doubtful that men have ever really liked the poetry of Emily Dickinson. During her lifetime no man admired it, though a number of women gave her generous and understanding praise. Since her death, and particularly in the last few years, there has been a good deal of scholarly exploitation. But persistent misreading cannot be called a proof of admiration. On the contrary, it suggests a deep unconscious dislike for the person the poetry expresses and a strong desire to put her down. All her male readers appear to repeat the experience of Higginson, who never liked her. He would have helped publish her poems if she had flattered him sexually, but this she was unable to do. And women, whom she could have flattered, had not then or now any power or cohesion as a sex or any loyalty to their own.

The circle of tragedy was complete. To save her talent from destruction, she turned from the male, and, since love she must, loved two brilliant and fascinating women who for a time gave her poetry their warm support. When the second love failed in its turn, she wrote her great tortured poems and made one tentative step toward publication. Higginson did not so much rebuff her as give her time to reconsider, and her decision was to write only for private relief. Dying, she abandoned her poetry to its fate, and it has been a curious one. Dribbled out over a half-century and more, misedited, misinterpreted, maliciously attacked, it has still one challenge to meet. If the scattered bits are ever brought together in a coherent whole and perceived as a whole, it might go to the bonfire with Sappho's and only a few puzzling and brilliant lines be handed down to be admired and misinterpreted a thousand years hence.

High School Crack-up

Esther Newton

Part 1

This paper grew out of an odd discomfort which several women experienced while reading *Zelda*, the biography of Zelda Fitzgerald. Zelda was diagnosed as mentally ill, and confined for many years in various institutions. Several of us women agreed, however, that her letters seemed coherent and insightful, rather than what we thought of as crazy (confused, deluded ravings). How could a supposedly hopeless schizophrenic write clear, if angry letters, let alone a novel?

It was in one of these letters, I think, that Zelda told Scott that her only alternative to marriage with him was madness. He didn't take her seriously, and waited impatiently for her return to a "normal" life with him.

As I was puzzling over Zelda's life, I happened to read *The Four-Gated City* by Doris Lessing. Lynda Coldridge, one of the central characters, went insane shortly after her marriage, and was hospitalized. Later, she lived in the same house with her husband, but insisted she was too "ill" to be touched by him. Whenever her husband suggested that Lynda should become his wife again, her response was another "psychotic" episode, and back to the hospital.

I began to count up female characters (as portrayed by women) and women authors or artists who went insane and/or attempted suicide. My list looked like this:

Zelda (suicide attempt, insanity), Lynda Coldridge (suicide attempt, insanity), Sylvia Plath (insanity, suicide), Virginia Woolf (insanity, suicide), *The Snake Pit* (insanity), *I Never Promised You a Rose Garden* (insanity), Jill Johnston (insanity), Edna Pontellier in *The Awakening* (suicide), Marilyn Monroe, Janis Joplin, Dianne Arbus (the photographer) (all suicide), Yvonne Rainer (the choreographer and dancer) and Dorothy Parker (suicide attempts). I'm sure you all can think of others; those are just the women who came to my mind right away.

I also thought of some exceptions: Anais Nin (although she suffered from serious depressions), Gertrude Stein, whose life is suggestive and needs further thinking out, and Valerie Solanis. Some of my women students said that "The Scum Manifesto" sounded crazy to them. We all agreed it was coherent, however. It is this kind of crazyness that I want to talk about then. The "Scum Manifesto" is like an armor-plated descendent of Zelda's letters to Scott, so I'm back where I started.

I found a suggestive interpretation of insanity and a truck load of data in *Sanity, Madness and the Family*, by Laing and Esterson. The book opens with the same question I had been asking: "are the experience and behavior that psychiatrists take as symptoms and signs of schizophrenia more socially intelligible than has come to be supposed?" (p.13) The authors explore the problem by interviewing eleven schizophrenic hospitalized women with their families. Simply, the authors concluded that much of so-called schizophrenic behavior is a predictable and purposeful response to certain techniques of mental torture. By the time I finished the book my head was swimming, not with the supposed insanity of the women, but with the insanity of their families, any family, my family.

Some of the mental tortures imposed on the "crazy" women by their families were: denial, restriction of autonomy, fusion with the mother, paranoia (usually the father's) regarding the sexual intentions of other men, mystification, contradiciton (double-bind), and tabued areas. I'll explain these later.

A composite list of the women's "sick" symptoms were: "cheeky" (hostile, disobedient) towards parents, hears voices, hears others' thoughts, others hear her thoughts, hallucinations, paranoia, coma, refusal to eat, preoccupation with sexual fantasies, has bomb inside her which is dangerous to others, can't mix in "crowds," believes parents and husband are dead, impulsive aggressive behavior, woolly, vague, confused thought processes. Suicidal. Preoccupation with religious ideas.

The families keep saying over and over to the interviewers: "I don't know what happened to her. She used to be, before her illness, happy, cheerful, no trouble to anyone, obeyed all our commands," etc. This is "normality." To be ill is to be miserable, unhappy, quarrelsome, disobedient, have sexual fantasies, to blame, reproach, want to get away from family—husband, try to kill herself, etc.

Laing and Esterson suggest that the schizophrenic women are most crushed when considered most normal by their families, and most alive when considered most "crazy." Caught in an intolerable, frozen normality, these women resorted to behavior which was then labeled insane, basically an attempt to leave the scene of the action, the "real" world, and retreat to an interior self. Also the women made devious attempts to express their rage. Then too, the "illness" caused the parents to send the daughters to mental hospitals, so the daughters "escaped" physically.

Suppose then that the *families* of these eleven women were insane. The women never had a chance; most never even got married, (the usual out for women, even if it is out of the frying pan into the fire). They certainly never produced anything, because they became "ill" in their teens and never recovered. Like most of us women, they were unsung and unrecognized.

But what about Sylvia Plath and Virginia Woolf and Zelda? They got away from their families, out into the "real" male world, and were even praised and pampered. Yet their work reads like the statements of the unsung women. And the end, although delayed, was the same. The conclusion I draw from this is that the "real" world out there is like a big family which is making us "ill," using those same techniques of mental torture. As a result, we women are always struggling, in our own minds and with each other, between a false and crushing "normality" and a self-destructive but defiant "madness."

Look how this works out:

Denial: we are told that we are silly, irrational, stupid, fit only for fucking, etc. But if we confront these accusations we are told it is our imagination; or, that our roles are complementary to men's roles, different, not inferior. We sometimes sense that men hate and fear us; but are told this is not true. Our experience is continually denied, invalidated, made invisible.

Restriction of autonomy: need anything be said here? Women

45

should stay at home, we are only Mrs. so and so, not persons in our own right, we should not travel, not be out in the world, not work, not be independent, not support selves, etc.

Fusion with mother: women should be traditional, just like mothers. Women *are* mothers. However, a contradiction operates here. We should be the opposite of our mothers: not frigid like her, not bitchy like her, not nagging like her.

Paranoid fears of men (sex) derived from fathers: in my experience, these fears are not all that paranoid. Also, men's sexuality is misrepresented to us via macho myths.

Mystification: women denied knowledge about how the world, things, work. We are mystified about our own bodies, about our roles, about our enemies.

Contradiction (double-bind): see above under fusion with mother. Or, be a sex-pot/be a virgin . . . Be attractive to all men/if men are attracted to you you're a slut . . . be bright/don't use your mind . . . you women are so dependent!/don't be a ball-breaking bitch! etc. etc.

Tabued areas: (this refers to experience which cannot be discussed), sexuality, lesbianism, anger, aggression, autonomy.

The women artists, then are symbolizing, and living out, the general condition of women. However, they tend to be crazy-suicidal rather than crushed-normal, for two reasons. The first has to do with the occupational hazards of writing and creating. In order to write authentically, a person has to look inside herself, set up an interior dialogue similar to that of the schizophrenic women. Clearly what many women artists find is their ground-up rage and confusion. Secondly, becoming an artist, becoming recognized, separates women from the "normal" world of other women. When you read the lives of women artists, you see a variety of ways, some more successful than others, in which these women tried to adapt to their special status. (For instance, Gertrude Stein wrote, in her early novel, *Q.E.D.*, "Thank god I was not born a woman.")

For myself, I do not want to be what parents, men, the "real" world says I am or should be. But I don't want to be "crazy" or kill myself, either. This means accepting all my past selves: the me who tried and failed to be "normal," the me who went "crazy" and came back. It means figuring out what my experience means, and who I am, for myself. In that spirit, I want to write about a part of my past which is not so painful to me now as it was, and which may speak to the experience of other women.

Part 2

For two months in 1956, before and after my sixteenth birthday, I kept a journal. When the journal began, I was functioning "normally" in the "real" world: I was dating boys, eating dinner with my family, going to school, getting good grades, and doing my homework. In my journal, I recorded my inner thoughts and daily concerns. My secrets included increasing signs of "madness": outbursts of rage, staying more and more in my room, self hatred, self mutilation and confusion. In the last entries I was no longer able to keep my "madness" secret.

I grew up in New York City during the 1940s. My environment was middle to upper middle class, mainly Jewish, and liberal to radical. I was sent to a small progressive school which pushed the then latest techniques in education, among them a less rigid notion of sex role stereotyping than was then common.

When I was 12, my mother, following a painful divorce, took me out to a Northern California suburb, where we both lived with her mother. I was put in public junior high school, and then high school. By the time I was sixteen, I had suffered through four years of public schooling and had arrived in the junior year of high school. The public school was agonizing for me, yet I had internalized most of its values, and blamed myself mercilessly for my inability to "really" fit in. My mother, who had her own troubles, and feared that I would move back East with my father, did little to encourage my feeble efforts at rebellion. My girl firends, never having known anything different, were more effectively resigned, i.e. more "normal" than I.

My high school offered basic training in oppression: child oppression (all teachers were superior to all students), sex oppression (all males were better than all females), popularity oppression (a student caste system modeled after, but different from the adult social classes) and race oppression (Blacks and Mexicans were simply not social persons).

Child oppression: The school was compulsory, regimented, competitive and effective. Children were at the mercy of teachers, whose rule, however, was disguised as benign, "in our interests," etc. Student government was a puppet popularity poll with no power; this may have been just as well, considering the values of the students. And of course all children (but girls more than boys) were controlled by their parents, on whom they were financially and emotionally dependent.

Sex oppression: As far as the school was concerned, boys and girls were technically equal. However, sex role differences were strictly enforced in toilets, dress regulations, athletics, shop versus cooking, etc. From the student viewpoint, boys and girls lived in two completely separate worlds. Male domination was unquestioned. Inter- and intra-sex behavior was endlessly discussed, and rigidly controlled down to the smallest and most personal detail. Heterosexuality was the only acceptable sex (although some boys, I now suspected, exploited others homosexually). From the girls' perspective, boys inhabited a mysterious, glamorous, free, and of course superior world from ours. To gain access to this world, via a boy friend, was *the* goal of existence. Not to have a boy friend was the worst possible fate.

Popularity oppression: The caste system was an outgrowth of male domination, for it was based on a hierarchy among boys; girls were ranked according to which caste of boys they dated. Beyond the pale were those girls who were said to fuck "anybody." Fucking even a popular boy made a girl lose reputation. Most girls who were said to fuck, whom we discussed in giggly whispers, were working class or Mexican girls.

The upper caste of most popular boys consisted of the good athletes, who were also "handsome and "good dressers." The middle caste was made up of the majority of boys who weren't popular but who didn't stick out either. The lower caste were called the "queers": these boys were physically handicapped, grossly "emotionally disturbed," the overly studious, the anti-social and obvious sex role deviants. The black and Mexican boys were not considered.

The girls' hierarchy was exactly parallel, except that membership in the popular caste was not based on any form of achievement, but on dating the popular boys. This depended on clothes, looks, and a mysterious something called "personality." A girl's "reputation" was her assessed value in the caste hierarchy.

When I say caste, I mean just that. There was no *open* dating or socializing between the castes, and it was extremely difficult to change your caste position. The lower castes were required to avoid and defer to the upper ones. The system was enforced by sadistic forms of social control, involving restriction of information, the power, through student government and influence, to define who was who and what was what, ridicule, gossip, and occasionally, physical force.

The dating system embodied the miserable status of the female students. To begin with, boys did not need to date; they could maintain respect and even be popular without dating at all. Dating for girls was mandatory; a girl had no social personality if she did not date, she was simply a social reject. So most girls were obsessed with dating and crushes, i.e., "boy crazy."

However, girls could take no initiative in getting dates. They strove to be "atractive" to boys. But the boy had to make the first move. Girls were not supposed to phone boys or ask boys for dates. Even the power to refuse boys who asked them was limited by the need to date, anyone. Once on a date, girls were supposed to "keep a boy interested," that is to be sexually available, but no to "go too far." A girl who did this got a bad reputation. On the other hand, a girl who would not "put out" at all, who was "frigid" also got a bad reputation.

"Normal" behavior for me meant being who the school wanted me to be: bright, obedient female student; who the other students thought I was: a big, awkward, badly dressed, too studious girl hanging desperately on the tag end of the middle caste. And who my mother and grandmother thought I should be but wasn't: a bright, charming, helpful, co-operative daughter and granddaughter.

I might add that my family, while in retrospect no crazier than most others, was culturally deviant. I lived with my mother and grandmother. There were never any men in the house. My father, long divorced from my mother, lived far away in New York. I was hopelessly entangled in a power struggle between them, and terriby confused about what was going on and where my loyalties should lie.

Who did I think I was, in the middle of all this? I didn't know. My journal referred to my other life in the East, where I returned each summer, and where I was more respected. Meanwhile I tried desperately to counter the negative judgements that were imposed on me. School: you're a girl, not good for much, but you're not as obedient as a girl should be, and too smart. Mother: you're not obedient, not charming, you're ungrateful. Students: you're a girl, you're unpopular, you're ugly, you're too smart and too athletic.

The only sources of support were good grades, occasional comfort from one or two girl friends, and extensive help from one woman teacher. Just like the families of the schizophrenic women, the "real" world insisted that *I* was the bad one, *they* were all fine.

The journal, the only ear which I trusted completely, showed my secrets to be full of obsessions, confusions, fantasies, as well as many authentic insights which I wasn't any too confident about at the time.

School, where I got good grades, was even so a source of confusion:

> "I didn't do one lick of homework this weekend, and it was a great mistake. I'll really be sorry. What's the matter with me?? Have I no will power? I wish I could quit school. It seems so unrealistic, so far from life."

The journal is mainly concerned with three topics: boys, the power struggle with my mother, and girl friends.

My fantasies about boys were endless. I listed over and over my past crushes on boys I hardly knew, against a background of my current crush on another boy I hardly knew:

> "I knew it. It turned out that John *was* at Performers on Friday. He played a big old solo. I probably could have had him all evening. Of course he won't show up again for months. And I was at Miss White's! Oh well, it's probably just as well. There is no doubt that I am attracted to him, and there's no sense fanning the flames that can only lead to hopelessness. Poor John, he doesn't realize what a little love could do for him. I guess it's not my problem. I wish it was."

In between this kind of thing are wistful references to relationships with boys in the East, some of which seemed more "real" to me. As to the boys I actually dated, I was sadly analytic, but had no answers to the questions raised by my experience. Notice how many "guesses" I had to make:

"In the middle of the 8th grade I met Paul at (dancing school). From the moment I met him I was out to get him. I liked him at first I guess. But I guess for my ego I was just determined to get him. And I certainly did. For a year we went together, and for the last two months of it we went steady. I knew I didn't like him when I accepted his offer to go steady. I mean I liked him but not sexually. He bored me, for my mind out-stripped his by about 50 miles. He was smart, but I was smarter. Furthermore, my personality was much stronger and more forceful. I gave in to him a lot to try to hide this, but it really was pathetically obvious.

Also, he never kissed me. We held hands and danced close, but he never kissed me. I guess he would have gotten around to it eventually, but he was scared I guess. And I don't think the match was too popular with his friends. He was really pretty cute, and I guess everyone wondered why he was going with me. The only reason that I went steady with him was that I wanted to find out what it was like to go steady, and there was so much security in it. Also going with him brought my reputation up a lot."

and again:

"I have just spent a more or less enjoyable evening with Ed. Ed really is a nice boy . . . but for some reason I don't go for Ed in a romantic way. I feel sorry for him, because he really likes me. I wonder if he dreams about me the way I dream about boys I like? It is a rather frightening thought. With Ed, everything is so false. That's the way it has been with almost all the boys I have ever known. There have been damned few exceptions . . . I never really fell for Paul, and he was one of the first on my list of lies. Poor boy, I fooled him so shamefully. I am such a sham, and why they don't realize it I'll never know . . . Bob was and still is the best example of sham. Now I am beginning to think that he was fooling me as much as I was fooling him. Isn't it ridiculous. But he wanted something, sex. That isn't what I wanted, but it's what I wound up with."

I had moments of painful clarity about the popularity caste system, and how angry I was about it. But I had largely accepted its negative view of me. Nor did I question male superiority, confining myself, consciously to envy of the popular *girls*.

Fighting with my mother reached a peak at this time. I was striving for a degree of autonomy which threatened her need to keep me with her. At the same time, I felt terribly guilty and confused about our fights. The events in the drama were complicated. Mothers, it seems, have more direct power over us than anyone else, but that is not the subject of this paper. I see better now what the "real" world had done

51

to her. I can afford this luxury since she now longer has the power (or burden) of being responsible for my life. One fight may give some of the flavor, if not the substance. One of the issues was the use of her car. In California it is impossible to get anywhere without a car. Bicycles were tabu:

> "Last night the car only set it off. The spark was: I said rather cuttingly that there was nothing to do around here but brood. At this point my mother started fooling around with her wispy hair, and looking very smug. 'You are much too given to brooding,' says she in her most superior. I cannot really explain why this made me so furious . . . "

I could not have managed without my girl friends, but some of my friendships were not so friendly:

> "This deal with Anne is really beginning to reach the ridiculous stage. And I am beginning to hate myself more than Anne or anyone else. I am acting like a first class hypocrite. And I can't really figure her out. I don't know how much she likes me, or if she does at all, or if she is completely out of herself. One thing is sure, she hurts often, and with an apparently clear conscience. She makes an ass out of me with John. I think the only real solution is to try to keep away from both of them."

But,

> "Actually it's a good thing for me that she is there, because she is the only one I can go around with during lunch. Of course she's in the same predicament, but she can always cup it up to someone. And I hate myself for cutting her so much to Cassandra while still being friendly with her. I am doing just what I hate and complain of in others. I wish I could get out of this mess. But I don't quite know how."

At the same time, I sometimes felt attracted to my girl friends, which scared me speechless. This subject was absolutely tabu, so whatever I felt was *my fault*. There was no way to find out what others felt. After a fight with Anne, mentioned above, I wrote:

> "Either she adores me, or she needs a friend or she admires me. I suspect it's a little of all three. I don't think she will stay mad. If I were a boy she would go ape over me. I have just come to an important point. She knows, and I know, that something is sort of odd about our relationship. I wonder sometimes if I am a homosexual. If I am, then why do I get crushes on boys?"

Later on, a crush on a older girl was rationalized away:

> "I have figured out my 'thing' about Judy. I don't really think of her as a person, but as an impersonal symbol of the kind of intellectual,

intelligent person I wish I were. She is just a symbol to me, and I don't think of her in terms of reality, but in terms of an idea or ideal. I feel better now that I have it straightened out in my mind."

The shadow fell in secret, the day after my 16th birthday, a month after I began the journal:

"After school I went to the dentist and got lots of novacain. When I came home my jaw was completely out. I decided to take a razor blade and find out how much I couldn't feel . . . I gashed myself quite deliberately in the chin. In fact, I carved it quite carefully. I passed it off pretty well as an accident with my mother and others. And I satisfied all my desires . . . after dinner my mother and I went to see the "Desk Set" which was very good."

During the Christmas vacation, I flew back East, over my mother's attempts to prevent me, and had what I thought was a wonderful time. When I got back, I found I could no longer live in the "real" world. I wrote that "everything hurts," that there was nothing real in me but a "small shrine at the center, very small and very strong."

"Tonight I sat down on the couch and as I sat back I accidentally leaned against the dog. I turned around to say 'excuse me' and out of a clear blue sky she bit me on the nose (that was what was sticking out I guess). I grabbed her neck and started to shake her. Suddenly I let go as tears came to my eyes. I don't know why. She didn't hurt me much. All of a sudden I felt terrible. I staggered upstairs and fell on the floor crying and sobbing. I guess the dam just broke or something. I cry pretty often alone, but I die when I cry in front of people. I even feel guilty crying alone. I keep wanting to drive my fist through a window. I have a very strong wish to do it. Partly for attention and partly to hurt myself. I wish I wasn't so God damn alone and confused and crazy."

That night I dreamed a long and terrible dream, of chasing and being chased, and in the dream I had a beard. For a moment when I woke up, I wasn't sure whether I was a boy or a girl. In the last paragraph of the journal, I reflected on an apppointment with the hair dresser the next day:

". . . my hair gives me a sense of camoflage and protection. I am torn between a desire to have it cut short, and a desire to keep up pretenses as much as possible. I don't know how I'll have it cut. I am feeling so defiant, I feel like having it all cut off as short as possible, just to show that I don't give a damn. There's more to say, but to hell with it."

In the next few days I began to break windows in the house, threaten my mother, drink to unconsciousness, fly into uncontrollable rages and tears, etc. My mother thought to commit me to a local hospital. If she had, perhaps I would have wound up like the schizophrenic women in *Sanity, Madness and the Family*. But, partly through the intervention of the sympathetic woman teacher, I was sent to a therapist instead. With the help of the therapist and the teacher, I was able somehow to get through the rest of the school year, although there were frequent outbursts of my "sickness."

At the end of the year, I went back East and never returned to California again, except to visit. My father sent me to a boarding school, where the "real" world was less destructive. Gradually, with help, I repaired myself. But there won't be peace between me and the "real" world until the "real" world is a saner place for me (and other women) to live in.

The Vision and Persecution of Aurora Phelps

Arlene Kisner, Lois Hart, Ellen Shumsky

What follows is the chronological documentation of a woman's struggle to create a Woman's Community. In 1891, Aurora H. C. Phelps petitioned the Massachusetts legislature to enact a charter mandating the establishment of a matriarchal community. She and her associates incorporated under the name *Woman's Economical Garden Homestead League*. This corporation was to administer and manage funds to secure for working women and minors a "liberal industrial education and the establishment of an industrial Homestead Settlement." Aurora fervently believed that in addition to the inalienable rights of life, liberty and happiness, every woman had a right to an independent garden home controlled by and transferred to women only. She endeavored for five years to make this paper matriarchy a reality. Originally lauded by the press as "not a ranting, rabid woman's rights advocate," her image was rapidly escalated into that of a paranoid Amazon guilty of chronic "fractiousness" as she was driven to defend her buildings and land by force of arms—a warfare that culminated in her murder. It was only by slimmest chance that we discovered Aurora Phelps and her episode in herstory. We hope the intact newspaper accounts will convey the martyrdom of this visionary feminist.

From the *Woburn Advertiser*—July 28, 1871
WOMEN'S HOMESTEAD LEAGUE:

Mrs. Aurora H. Phelps has bonded in Woburn and East Stoughton 26 lots of land for dwelling-house purposes in connection with this League and as soon as arrangements can be made will commence building in detail. Subscription books will be sent around for aid and offerings as low as 5¢ will be thankfully received. The scheme is considered by many a perfectly feasible one; that its purposes are good nobody can deny. We learn the above from the *Boston Times*.

From the *Woburn Advertiser*—September 16, 1873
HOMESTEAD LEAGUE:

Miss Aurora H. C. Phelps seems at last to be in a fair way to accomplish her long wished-for project of establishing cheap homes for working women. Last Thursday she broke the first ground for a village at Woburn, and it is proposed at once to erect a laundry. The land lies between the Lowell Railroad track and Beach Street, and comprises about 60 acres. The league is formed under a statute of the State, and may be composed of any number of members, who can hold property to an amount not exceeding $200,000, which if owned by females is exempt from taxation. If a member holding property dies it descends in the female line, just as in England male succession is the law.

We heartily approve of this enterprise, as not only likely to add much to the prosperity of the town, but to ameliorate the condition of laboring women, and hope the project will receive all encouragement. Miss Phelps is not one of the ranting, rabid women's rights advocates, and undertakes this task merely to better the condition of poor women . . . Miss Phelps will make Woburn her home, although the head-quarters of the League are established by law at Boston.

From the *Woburn Journal*—October 18, 1873
AURORA VILLAGE:

Upon a recent visit to the proposed site of the above village, we found that the cellar for the laundry was ready for the building and the workmen told us that it was Miss Phelps' intention to have a dozen houses erected this fall. Time, money and perserverance will work wonders.

From the *Woburn Advertiser*—October 24, 1873
AURORA VILLAGE:

The frame for the first building was raised on Wednesday, October 22, 1873. The building is to be 60 x 25 ft., 3½ stories high and to be used for a laundry. Miss Phelps called the attention of those present to the nature of the philanthropic enterprise in which she is engaged for the purpose of raising and assisting the poorer classes. She christianed it Bethesda, a Hebrew word meaning house of mercy. She expects to have several dwelling houses up in the fall.

From the *Woburn Advertiser*—November 14, 1873
BETHESDA LAUNDRY:
A fund-raising benefit, the Woburn Bazaar, will be held on November 25th, at 192 Main Street.

From the *Woburn Advertiser*—December 16, 1873
BETHESDA LAUNDRY:
It appears that the Bethesda Laundry started by Miss Phelps at the incipient Aurora village has not prospered as we had hoped from the start it might. It is at present in the hands of the Sheriff, there being two attachments upon it, one from Mr. Jacob Whitcher for lumber, and another from the Boston and Lowell Railroad company for transportation; also one or more carpenter's liens. We hope Miss Phelps may be able to extricate herself from her present unpleasant position and carry out the enterprise she had undertaken.

From the *Woburn Journal*—December 27, 1873
The land secured for a woman's homestead and industrial settlement comprising about 60 acres . . . . The property is worth $15 or $20,000. There is a mortgage of $2,000 due next August, and other debts that mount to about $3,000. While not a charity or a philanthropy, this endeavor will be a refuge for the distressed. An industrial school, a co-operative table and bakery are planned to begin soon. Rent of homes applies as payment on homesteads, and great pains will be taken to introduce other skilled industries for the immediate benefit of the women and men residing in or near the women's village . . . .

From the *Boston Globe* —October 23, 1874
BETHESDA LAUNDRY:
The scheme of Mrs. Aurora H.C. Phelps presenting to the weak sex of New England advantages and protection which was not previously enjoyed, was yesterday brought nearer its realization by the raising of the first building in the prospective community . . . . Phelps made a

speech crediting the working women and men for work completed, she threw a bottle of water (that had a J.C. Hennessy cast) at the building and christened it Bethesda. The fact that the bottle thrown within a rod of the building, struck a pile of boards about a rod one side of the frame, called forth a well-fitted remark "A woman never could throw a stone." The title of "Bethesda" is well adapted to the building inasmuch as therein or (in the vicinity) it is proposed to wash away not only the stains from soiled garments, but also the marks of tyranny from the souls of women. . . .

From the *Woburn Advertiser*—July 1, 1875
GRAND UPRISING OF THE AMAZONS:

Quite a little breeze has been stirred up in town by an affair which occured at Aurora Village eastside Monday evening. It appears that there has been some question as to the title by which Miss Aurora H.C. Phelps holds certain land in the easterly part of the town on which she has caused to be erected the Bethesda Laundry, so-called. The merits of the dispute we do not understand and there are very few of sufficient legal ability to comprehend it. But it seems that Miss Phelps is determined to hold possession of the property at all hazards and against all claimants and has armed and fortified herself and retainers to meet and repel any invasion of the sacred soil. Monday evening, Mr. Charles Hart of Hart and Co., express, accompanied by another man took up a case of muskets to the laundry for Miss Phelps, the express charges on which were $1.75; the instructions were not to deliver them unless the full charges were paid. Miss Phelps appeared armed with 3 pistols which she carried in a sash fashioned around her waist. She tendered $1.50 in payment of the charges, which Mr. Hart declined to receive and refused to leave the muskets unless the full bill was paid. Aurora drew a pistol and pointed at Mr. Hart and ordered him to leave the box, which after some half hour's parley with the belligerent Queen of the Amazons he did. It has been stated that the muskets in question came from the State arsenal at Framingham and if so, they must have been sent by order of the Governor or Adjutant General. This, however, we are a little disposed to doubt. Whether this is to be the end of the matter between Mr. Hart and Aurora we are not definitely informed. Several attempts have been made to fire the laundry within a short time and we have been informed by an insurance agent that policies of insurance on it have been cancelled.

From the *Woburn Advertiser*—July 8, 1875
THE WAR IN THE EAST:
The selectmen considered the matter of Aurora's guns of sufficient importance to take action upon, and Friday morning at a meeting they decided to send a delegation to Adjutant General Cunningham to secure the removal of the offensive weapons. This was agreed to by him or his assistant and Friday afternoon, a deputy came out to Woburn, went over to the laundry with Chief of Police Mann and two officers. Miss Phelps was away, but the woman in charge refused to deliver the guns or open the door. The police broke open the door, secured the guns and they were returned to the city in the evening. The woman spoke her mind quite freely to the deputy. She said it was all nonsense to take the guns away, that they would be sent back again and that Miss Phelps had got to have them. One of the officers offered to stop with them nights and protect them. She soured on him in a minute and told him that they didn't want any of his protection, "they were not going to bring up poor soldier's orphans to be protected by such rogues as he." The war is probably over.

From the *Woburn Advertiser*—July 15, 1875
THE PERSECUTION OF AURORA PHELPS:
Friends of Miss Aurora H.C. Phelps, who called on her at the Bethesda Laundry in Woburn yesterday found her extremely ill, it is alleged, from the effects of poison. On Monday of last week she was indisposed and took two doses of a tonic which she kept in the house. On that eve, or the next morning, as was alleged, she was seized with spasms, and a Doctor sent for, who pronounced the symptoms like those produced by arsenic. He also analyzed the tonic and it is alleged arsenic was found in this. A small box marked arsenic was found, it is said, knowledge of which was not previously possessed by Miss Phelps. The affair is a profound mystery to her friends. She is in very critical condition and her recovery is said to be doubtful.
Dr. S.W. Kelly, the Physician in attendance upon Miss Phelps having been shown the above statement pronounces it entirely

unfounded. He never has analyzed any tonic or discovered any arsenic; neither has Miss Phelps manifested any symptoms or being under the influence of poison of any kind. He pronounces her case one of weakness and debility caused by lack of proper attendance and food. So far as the idea of their being a disposition on the part of the citizens of Woburn to persecute Miss Phelps is concerned, it is mere moonshine. Miss Phelps is entitled to and will receive the protection of all her rights under the law the same as any other person in town.

From the *Boston Daily Globe*—July 22, 1875
The Bethesda Laundry place was sold under the name of John Nelson to L.G. Richardson for the town, the unpaid taxes being $101.91.

From the *Boston Daily Globe*—July 24, 1875
THE LAUNDRY WAR:
Miss Aurora H.C. Phelps is again in trouble having opened hostilities with Mr. John Nelson who claims never to have been paid for the land on which the laundry building stands, while Aurora says she did pay for it. Nelson went in and cut the hay on the land. Phelps and her forces (two women and a man) harassed him but he gathered half the hay and left the rest. The next morning it was gone. He came back the following day with reinforcements hoping by force of numbers to harvest the whole crop. An interesting little squabble may result for whatever may be said of Miss Phelps otherwise, she certainly is plucky.

From the *Boston Daily Globe*—July 26, 1975
A party headed by the Chief of Police and John Nelson went over to Bethesda Laundry Saturday and brought away two loads of hay. The force was too strong for Aurora and she submitted without making any resistance.

From the *Woburn Advertiser*—July 29, 1875
THE DIFFICULTY IN MAKING HAY:
The fair denizen of Bethesda Laundry is, we fear, in a state of chronic fractiousness. This time she has her quarrel with John Nelson,

of whom she bought her land at Aurora Village and who still claims ownership of the same. Nelson disposed of some standing grass on the premises last week to a party by the name of Tuttle, but when Tuttle went over to mow his grass last Wednesday, he was met by one of Aurora's Bodyguards who ordered him away and enforced the order by showing a revolver. Tuttle reported the episode to Nelson and the next day they faced the music together. There was the same bellicose exhibition but this time it failed of its purpose for Nelson stood his ground. The grass, or a portion of it, was mown and raked and left at nite in cocks upon the field of battle. Friday morning, Nelson went to resume operations but lo! his hay had gone. During the nite it had taken to itself wings and flown where no man listeth. He desisted on account of rain from further proceedings in the hay business and recruited his army. Saturday, Chief of Police Mann, Tuttle, two reporters, Nelson and some harvesters advanced upon the laundry. The force was too strong for her ladyship and she made no demonstration. The work progressed in quiet and the hay is all harvested.

From the *Woburn Advertiser*—August 5, 1875
ALAS POOR YORICK:
Aurora H.C. Phelps has been writing letters to Selectmen again. Saturday they received a long message requesting them to send her provisions, as she was without the necessaries of life. From the articles specified one might judge that she had changed her laundry into a "meals-at-all hours" place. The town fathers sent her some things with which to sustain life and notified the city of Boston of the case, where it is supposed she has a legal residence. Perhaps this will result in the removal of Aurora to another burgh.

The laundry estate Aurora Village has been leased by John Nelson to Charles Wendall and probably Miss Phelps will have to pack up willing or unwilling.

From the *Boston Daily Globe*—August 5, 1875
Aurora H.C. Phelps has been given food and clothing by the town of Woburn, which proposes however to make Boston pay for same.

From the *Boston Daily Globe*—August 6, 1875

Miss Aurora H.C. Phelps has been warned to vacate her fortress by Charles Wendell who leased the premises of Nelson, and she has only this week to remain, before final proceedings will be instituted to eject her, should she refuse to go.

From the *Boston Daily Globe*—August 12, 1875

Miss Aurora H.C. Phelps was represented by counsel Saturday in the case of her ejectment from the laundry property. Counsel represented that Miss Phelps was sick and couldn't be moved at present, and she was in consequence granted further time.

From the *Woburn Advertiser*—November 25, 1875
MISS PHELPS RISES TO EXPLAIN:
Sir:

About 2 years ago, John Nelson bought some lime, cement and bricks from me. He gave me an old stove in part payment; the balance, due for 2 barrels of cement, four of lime and several thousand bricks is yet unpaid. Today he came to my house asking to see me, saying the stove was his and he wanted it. I sent word he has no stove here; I was too ill to see him, if he had any business with me he must go to my lawyer. He left, threatening to bring a force to take it. Evidently he has forgotten that he is under legal process for unfulfilled contract and the theft and burglariously entering and robbing our house. I do not believe the town officers will wink at another mob under his control or lend themselves to his illegal lawsuits when they learn from your columns the real facts in this case. You have said you wish to give the truth. Please allow me a hearing in your paper as well as my enemies. (Woburn, Massachusettes, November 12, 1875. Respectfully, Aurora H.C. Phelps)

From the *Boston Daily Globe*—January 6, 1876
WOBURN—DEATH OF A NOTE CHARACTER:

After months of suffering, Miss Aurora H.C. Phelps died at the Bethesda Laundry, so called, on Tuesday evening. Her career was eventful, and the latest and best endeavors of her life were devoted to the amelioration of the condition of "lone, lorn women". The cause of her death was Brights' disease of the kidneys, but she attributed it to the poisoning of a spring near her residence by malicious persons. She was attended in her last moments by two or three intimate friends, but had few needful comforts, dying in abject poverty, and the expenses of her funeral will have to be borne by the town or the city of Boston unless some charitably disposed persons come forward with the necessary funds. The only articles which her room contained were a dilapidated bedstead, ragged bedclothes, two or three rickety chairs and a few books.

According to her own account, Miss Phelps was born about the year 1839-40, in a sleigh on the public road near the boundary line between Massachusettes and New York, while her parents were making a forced (?) journey. She claimed her home to be Elmira, New York and that when she was about 8 or 9 years old her parents went to Europe, taking her with them, where they remained about 2 years, when they returned to the United States. At the age of 12 she professed religion and joined the Baptist Church in Elmira, New York, remaining a constant member of the faith until quite recently.

When about 17 or 18 years old she went again to England with her parents, remaining abroad several years and while there became acquainted with and married an intimate personal friend of the late Charles Dickens (name unknown) by whom she had one child. Soon after her husband died, and she then returned to America and resumed her maiden name. She entered Oberlin college and afterwards the college at Galesburg, Illinois. During the rebellion she was a hospital nurse.

In 1871, she received from the legislature an act incorporating the "Woman's Homestead Garden League" together with Harriet R. Hunt and Elmira E. Gibson as coadjutors to the right to hold property to the value of $5000. She purchased of John Nelson a large tract of land bordering on the Boston and Lowell Railroad and near the Woburn watering station, Nelson giving her a bond for a deed; she immediately began the erection of a building to be used for laundry purposes, and had in contemplation the erection of other buildings for various purposes connected with the establishment.

The failure of her plans and her troubles since are well known and of late she has received aid from the town and also from the city of

Boston. She joined St Charles' Catholic Church in this town last July.

From the *Woburn Avertiser*—January 6, 1876

Miss Aurora H.C. Phelps who during the last 3 years has been, to an extent, unfavorably known to the people of Woburn, died at Bethesda Laundry, Tuesday evening at 7 after an illness which had confined her to her bed for the greater part of 6 months. At times she would rally and seem to be better and as late as Monday she was so far improved as to be able to be up and about the house for a time. Monday night and Tuesday she was somewhat worse but not sufficiently so to alarm her attendants. She passed quietly away and without apparent pain. The room in which she lived and died and in fact the whole building, is more like a barn than a place where humans should live. A rickety bed, covered with ragged bed clothing, a few chairs and other pieces of furniture and some personal effects of the room, and it looks cheerless indeed. Her complaint as stated by Dr. G.W. Gay of Boston and some of our resident physicians was Brights' disease of the kidneys, although Miss Phelps claimed that it was in consequence of drinking poison. About the middle of July last she applied to the town for relief and since that time she has been supported by the town although her legal residence is in Boston.

She stated to the writer sometime before her death that she was in want of nothing and could attend to her complaint as well as any doctors, she having studied for a doctress at an earlier period of her life. She therefore refused to see the town physicians. But little is known of her life before she commenced her public career. In carrying out her various schemes she had at different times received the attention of the legislature of the state and also been familiar with many of its first men, even Wilson. Miss Phelps we believe, has labored with the intention of ameliorating the condition of the unfortunate of her sex, but was regardless of the means she took to carry out her ideas. Her course since living in Woburn was not calculated to gain the confidence of the people, although she doubtless believed she was the victim of persecution. She received last summer the sacraments of the Catholic Church and became a communicant of that body. Earlier in life she became a member of the Baptist Church and entered upon a course of study with the intention of being a missionary. Miss Phelps' parents were residents of New York State, but she was born in Massachusettes. She travelled in Europe, had been married and leaves one son.

The estate is in a peculiar condition of which hardly anyone knows the ins and outs. Mr. John Nelson of whom she bought the place obtained some 2 months ago a verdict in a suit of ejectment before Judge Converse, but had not served a process. Miss Phelps had filed a suit in equity at Cambridge to compel the delivery of a deed she claimed was wrongfully withheld. This may or may not be continued by her legal representatives.

Her funeral takes place this afternoon. She leaves a will the contents of which are not yet known.

From the *Woburn Advertiser*—November 30, 1876
PHELPS ESTATE:
It will be remembered that at the time of her death Aurora H. C. Phelps was plaintiff in a suit against John Nelson to compel the conveyance of the Bethesda Laundry property which was under bond. Miss Phelps having died intestate, Josephine R.B. Bethuysen petitioned the Suffolk Probate Court to be appointed administratrix. The petition was dismissed and H. Burr Crandall appointed adminstrator. Afterwards the court appointed three appraisers. They found no personal or real property to appraise other than this claim to the laundry property, which claim could not be estimated. Monday the suit came up in the Superior Court for Suffolk County and the legal representatives of Miss Phelps not appearing they were non-suited and the property reverts to Mr. Nelson.

From the *Woburn Advertiser* —December 7, 1876
PHELPS ESTATE:
We have been requested to print the following:
In the suit between John Nelson and Aurora H.C. Phelps the action stands in court as it was at the time of her death and the property does not revert to Nelson as reported in last week's paper.

Return of the Amazon Mother

Jill Johnston

On an appointed day every spring parties of young Amazons and young Gargarensians met at the summit of the mountain which separated their territories and after performing a joint sacrifice spent two months enjoying promiscuous intercourse under cover of night. As soon as an Amazon found herself pregnant she returned home. Whatever girl children were born became Amazons and the boys were sent to the Gargarensians who because they had no means of ascertaining their paternity distributed them by lot among their huts. Modern Amazons are lesbians with or without children. Many contemporary lesbians are not spending two months of their excellent time fooling around at the summit with any Gargarensians, but some lesbians do want and have children and a number of lesbians are stuck with children they might not have had before the liberating effects of the Gay/Feminist revolutions. Whatever the circumstances it's a subject of some urgency to the lesbian community. Last February I shared a panel presentation with two other women at a Gay Activist Center in New York. It's a sensitive subject in which I'm still personally embroiled, but I felt a responsibility to unload my version of the problem for whatever it might contribute toward an ultimate variety of good solutions. I didn't think the whole audience was mothers and they weren't. I asked those who weren't if they were thinking of becoming lesbian mothers. Suddenly I wasn't sure why I was there. The other two women spoke first and they were very much into being just mothers. I had had a hazy idea we would all be getting together to celebrate the end of motherhood or something. But here were women who were proud mothers who were interested in sharing new ways of getting along as mothers bringing up their children with their female lovers and partners. Certainly I've advocated the lesbian communal household with its advantages of multiple parents for the children. It's easy recommending things you don't practically know anything about. My approach to life is completely historical. A wholesome and lofty attitude. Anyhow many women now are "coming out" (affirming their lesbian identity to themselves and others) after the aberration of a conventional marriage and a child or two and are faced with angry ex-husbands and parents and in-laws and poverty and the legal apparatus for taking their children away and the guilt of renouncing motherhood if they feel they *want* to give up their children or *have* to give up their children and the problems of living arrangements if they keep them, including most significantly the psychology of a coming-out in relation to the children. The legal problems for lesbian mothers who want to keep their children are critical. The courts rarely recognize the lesbian as a fit mother. Thus almost any father who has the desire and the means can take his child into custody away from a lesbian mother. A threat which retards the Gay revolution by keeping the woman a closet case. And which by the same token retards the evolution of finer mothers by suppressing the affirmation of sexual identity. Certainly when I was a younger woman at war with my sex role and without knowing it, I wasn't a fit mother by anybody's standards including my own and I had to let my children go to become myself. Certainly in any case none of us were told what a drastic drag it was to *be* a mother. I mean motherhood was a soft fuzzy-edge tinted photo of the young ageless beautiful cosmically fulfilled mother with her cooing dentine baby on the cover of one-a-them ladies' magazines. I didn't really believe that but I never thought it through and it was always the thing to do, especially if you didn't know what else to do and your mother thought you should go to a shrink. So I became a sort of pseudo-mother. I thought there were more mothers like that around. I mean mothers not archetypically the mothers, who somehow became mothers for a brief time. I am really a perennial daughter. Here is some history I relate to from Helen Diner's *Mothers and Amazons* published by Julian Press: "In time and reality, the Amazon kingdoms not only comprised an extremist end of matriarchy but also are a beginning and a purpose in themselves. Roaming daughter realms ... they markedly differ from the serenely tolerant mother clan as old as mankind, which pacifically exiled a young upstart manhood by exogamy. In the mother clan, there was a constant progression of great mothers begetting more great mothers. Amazons, however, reproduced the daughter type, which practically skips a generation and is something altogether different. They were conquerors, horse tamers, and huntresses who gave birth to children but did not nurse or rear them. They were an extreme, feminist wing of a young human race, whose other extreme consisted of the stringent patriarchies." By many accounts the Amazons did rear their daughters. By certain accounts the Amazons played a crucial historical role in the long bloody transition from the matriarchies to the patriarchies. No doubt we are presently at a juncture in history in which the Amazons return to perform a similar function as the transition is reversed. Anyway my mother and I were daughter types and probably my mother's mother was more like the mother in the procession of great mothers begetting more great mothers if that itself isn't a patriarchal fiction. Maybe the three of us were a squad of roaming daughters. The eldest did settle in one place and make the soup for her daughter and her granddaughter and grow up to be a shapeless old woman, so I think that's why I see her as the great mother type. My mother had no more business being a mother than I did without an Amazon community to support ourselves. Our time hadn't come yet. Our time has come. It's doubtless very satisfying to feel that we understand and approve the course of the grand drama of history. This is not the sort of thing the women at the lesbian mothers panel were interested in hearing about, about the antediluvian queens who're colonizing the world. The women who were at the panel are dealing with the law and the kitchen table. Each of the first two women who spoke lived with a lesbian lover and a child. One was very knowledgeable about the law problems I haven't thought much about. Although a feminist lawyer advised me and carried on for me last fall over the vaguely defined crisis of my son and his father who seemed embarrassed over the possibility of his son being identified as my son too and other complications, creating an either-or situation in which it seemed my son had to leave his house totally, be disowned as they used to say, or stay there and have nothing whatever to do with me. I had endless circular conversations with my feminist lawyer in which we were unable to resolve any action because I wanted to have my son and not eat him too as it were. I mean I didn't want custody and I wanted friendly communications including such events as being able to take him to a john lennon lawn party without having to abduct him for the occasion, which I did. Of course implicit behind the ultimatum to my son was a parallel ultimatum to me. That is, if you're not going to assume total responsibility as a mother then you can't scrape off the cream or play the visiting fireman the way of course 'so many fathers do. The ultimatum actually was a new and extreme version of a situation that existed ever since I had in fact abdicated my role as total mother: the restriction of my contact and communications with the children to their *father's terms only* in a constant atmosphere of unfriendliness or outright hostility calculated to arouse my guilt. The guilt of renouncing motherhood. A woman with my sort of history gets it both ways. I didn't give up my children as a lark. I was living in desperate circumstances alone with the children in a tenement either on welfare or on $25 a week from the father whenever it was forthcoming and trying to establish myself as a writer and have some sort of romantic and social life as well and I couldn't do it. If I wasn't ill I was screaming. The changeover was made gradually and irrevocably when the children's father felt reasonably secure with a new wife who apparently *wanted* to involve herself with her husband's children by another woman. I have to underscore here what should seem obvious by now, that the likelihood of a woman in my position receiving support at such a critical time from another mate, of either sex, was extremely dim, whereas a man in similar circumstances traditionally has very little trouble obtaining the services of a new slave mate. I would not have been looking for a slave in any case. That was understood to be the privilege of the man. Just a cooperative partner would have done nicely. But a woman fallen to the condition in which I found myself was something of an untouchable in our society and a cooperative partner was a consideration as remote as a ford foundation grant for an indigent mother of two. What I meant about getting it both ways is this, that I was socially culpable, both as a woman no longer with a husband and unable to sustain myself and two children adequately, and as a woman renouncing motherhood. And that now, as a woman better situated both materially and psychologically and in large part because I was able to pursue my own ends and development by that very act of delivering my children over to those better able to care for them, I am still blamed for my original defection and presented with obstacles in the way of the very contact and communications that now make more sense from my relatively liberated position. I think it's significant that in my case my son aligned himself with me in the classic revolt against the father and that my daughter as it looks right now appears to be a captive in her father's house. In the Amazon solution the daughters go with the mothers. Amazon or not we're involved in a Women's Revolution and it doesn't make much sense as mothers and sisters to go on handing ourselves over to the sons in sustenance and support no matter how much we like them (and I like mine) while the daughters continue to be prepared for another frustrating future as homemaker and sacrificial mother. I refer anybody to Virginia Woolf's *Room of One's Own* and *Three Guineas* for an eloquent account of the destitution of mothers and daughters and the urgent necessity of reestablishing that broken unity by which the daughters will be equipped financially and spiritually for independence and a broad gamut of options. This will not happen in any significant social sense until we see an end to the patriarchal nuclear family. Between me and my daughter stands the possessive father who needs the woman on all fronts to further his own traditionally sanctified ends. Certainly his daughter is more useful around the house than his son. Although I recognize an important bond of identity now well established between my daughter and her stepmother there is no reason except for an angry male why she can't have a relationship with me as well. Communications reached an all-time low during the past year when her father decided I was even more unsavory and disreputable than he thought I was at the time I rejected him as my domestic playmate. The lesbian mothers interested in remaining mothers and sharing new ways of getting along as mothers bringing up their children with their female lovers and partners are faced with the critical form of the discrimination I've experienced as a public lesbian. The law doesn't mean much in my case. My son was driven into an either-or choice, and my daughter successfully influenced to discredit me as a friend and sister. What's important about the law is the psychology behind

70

it. My ex-husband stepped up his antagonism toward me as a result of my public stance in the Lesbian/Feminist revolutions. The great legal apparatus of the nation stands behind him and gives him all the credibility he needs to nullify an already tenuous relationship and to drive his son into a social vacuum suspended as it were between the old but still ubiquitous estate of the oppressive authoritarian nuclear family and the new revolutionary hardly realized communal society of multiple parentage and a recognition of the rights and intelligence and autonomy of children. The law meant something a lot more concrete to the lesbian mothers at that panel. Here are a few statements made by the National Organization for Women in 1971 endorsing lesbianism as a feminist issue: "Married women are denied equality under laws that decree men as head of the household, but a wife is nonetheless allowed some legal protection. A lesbian, however, who shares her home with another woman—regardless of her income or responsiblities—foregoes all the economic and legal compensations granted to the married woman, including tax deductions, insurance benefits, inheritance rights, etc. . . . This prejudice against the lesbian is manifested in the courts as well. Whereas most divorced women are conceded the right to their children, a lesbian is automatically presumed unfit for motherhood, and can have her children taken away from her." In San Francisco a Lesbian Mothers Union is very active in agitating for legal aid as well as legal and psychological research for lesbian mothers and I've heard that a Union is being organized in Washington too. In San Francisco assistance is being solicited from mental health professionals to bring forward evidence for a test case in the courts. Much depends on undermining the strongly entrenched sickness theories of lesbianism perpetrated by the church and psychiatric profession in maintaining the status quo of the heterosexual institution. It is difficult to see how the male legal establishment can seriously recognize the rights of lesbian mothers when such recognition would amount to a stab in the back of the very patriarchal heterosexual system they are designed to protect. Lesbian motherhood is an affront to paternity and a denial of the assumed necessity of the male in any family structure. The nerve of illegitimacy was bad enough. Elizabeth Gould Davis, in her is book, *The First Sex*, wrote: "One of the most shocking lapses of morality, in the patriarchal view, is manifested in the birth of fatherless babies. Throughout the patriarchal age, women have suffered outrageously for this breach of male property rights, and their unfortunate babies have suffered even worse. Yet the only thing wrong with fatherless families, so deplored by present-day sociologists, is not that they are fatherless but that the mothers do not have the support and approval of society. For many millenia, in many parts of the world, women did, and still do, bring up very fine children without the help of men." Lesbian motherhood is a dramatic and more positive and for that reason I suppose more alarming variation of the unwed mother. The relative (assumed) sexual deprivation of the unwed mother is not such a threat to the established order of things. Lesbian motherhood as a phrase means I'm going to have my child and my sex too. My sex meaning both sex *per se* and my own sex—a double transgression. Behind the taboo and sickness theories of lesbianism is the acknowledged but unspoken challenge: a lesbian's prime commitment to another woman. The law, the church, the psychiatric professions are an interlocking triumvirate in defining the lesbian as illegal, evil, sick—in their respective terminologies, to legitimize discrimination in the interests of patriarchal dominion, making it very difficult for women to live in any primary relationship to each other. It's illegal in other words not to be in prime relationship to the male who defines the law by this very involvement. The legal right of the father to the mother. The case against lesbianism from the point of view of reproductive sexuality even if the society continues not to make certain technological discoveries available for reproductive purposes is as absurd as it was in the days of the Amazons, whose periodic excursions into a male community for the purpose of impregnating themselves didn't interfere with their freedom to do what they wanted sexually or in any other way. I mean there has never been a *necessary* connection between sexual habits or mores and reproductive sexuality. It is the modern woman captive by marriage in the patriarchal family who has been conditioned over centuries to see her reproductive sexuality in some necessary and essential connection of total lifestyle to the male with whom her occasional reproductive sexuality *might* be involved. *This* is absurd.

I was saying at the beginning of this essay that I went to that lesbian mothers panel with some hazy notion that we might be celebrating the end of motherhood. The other two women on the panel were as shocked by my position as I was taken aback by theirs. They made the conventional assumption for instance since I had willingly given up my children that I hated children. Even in a room full of lesbians I felt that old guilt about renouncing motherhood. It's one thing not to do it at all, but to do it and then to renounce it. . . . Well, what about the children, and so on. How could I say I felt ultimately I'd done my children a favor by letting them go. How could I explain the dynamic complexity of my responsibilities and my own needs and the double bind I was in and the impossibility of any really adequate solution at a time when there wasn't any such thing as a lesbian communal household and child-care centers were unheard of and even if they were, I was one who was a victim of the myth of motherhood. Motherhood as we know it now is an invention of the patriarchal property-oriented legal system. I think there is a natural kind of motherhood but we don't know too much about it coming as we do from artificial isolated nuclear structures. A basic conflict in my own situation was that I was instinctively constitutionally unable to "dominate" my children and yet I knew very well from all I had learned that as adults we were "superior" to children and were therefore required to teach and direct and discipline them. The conflict was so dramatic that the three of us I think were paralyzed by my inability to move decisively in one direction or the other. I was in fact extremely schizie. The way I've doped it out in retrospect is that one half of me was the internalized social father, or "parent," and the other half the instinctive communal nonauthoritarian mother, or "child." I was apparently close enough to the child to know that I was my own child so to speak and I never liked being taught directed and disciplined so how could I do it to these extensions of myself? On the other hand I had been socialized or educated along with the rest of my peers so I had a number of culturally imposed attitudes, a learned set as they say, which were real and believed and which operated in direct opposition to a deeper substratum of understood truth. At the heart of that learned set was the notion that kids were a special category of mobile vegetable. A whole species apart. Since we had been educated away from our original selves it makes sense that we would have forgotten who we were. I didn't see children as intelligences. Shulamith Firestone in *The Dialectic of Sex* has brilliantly described the gradual creation of an artificial state called "childhood" (a state of arrested psychic and social development)—and the segregation of children from the world of adults with whom they were originally integrated in the larger households or family communities, and with it the extension to absurd limits of woman's bondage to motherhood in the increased and exaggerated dependence of the children, who were systematically underestimated and regarded with a growing disrespect. The myth of childhood and the myth of motherhood are coeval and reciprocally interdependent creations. Neither would have been accomplished without privatization in the isolated nuclear family unit. My own condition was obscured to me in the giant privacy of my problem. I was unable to see that I was living the way I was because I was part of a severely oppressed class consisting of women and children. In privacy guilt multiplies and perpetuates its own reasons for justifying the oppressed condition. Had I had any political awareness I wouldn't have been trapped by the condition in the first place, I mean in the *double* oppression of adding children to my first problem of being a woman. With political awarness many women just stop having children. It seems to me that the lesbian mothers living in communal households are on the right track. I was naturally sympathetic with the lesbian mothers at the panel but disappointed in their imitation of the nuclear family model. I don't know if the women themselves, the "parents," were into role-playing in their relationships to each other, but I don't know how it's possible to avoid role-playing vis-a-vis the children in the nuclear unit which by its very nature is an authoritative hierarchical structure of oedipally (electra-ly) focused children and a projecting pair of parents. It is a propertied situation. A property is not an autonomous entity. We know that women and children were brought under greater and greater control through increased privacy in the nuclear unit. Private property. Keep off. The women at the panel did in fact sound to me like "parents" who were "bringing up children." As Firestone said, "the best way to raise a child is to LAY OFF." This is what I discovered *after* I let my children go. I didn't know how I could

74

communicate to the women at the panel the act of *psychic* dispossession that I experienced not too long after I had *physically* relieved myself. The revelation of course came from the children themselves. What they told me in essence was that they weren't children at all. They were seven and eight and they led me around one whole long summer's afternoon in the country through ravines cliffs waterfalls and tarzan swings in the woods communicating all the while by one symbolic act or another that they were perfectly conscious intelligent beings and in fact that they had always been so. I freaked out completely. I left them (they were staying with their grandmother) and drove to New York and couldn't make it. I called some friends who came halfway to rescue me. If children already knew everything, what did we know? Not much, I decided. I had clearly based my superiority on the knowledge of skills and the command of information. I had confused intelligence with skills and information. I decided that through education and coercion we as adults had moved into progressive states of specialized and highly operable ignorance—that the key to intelligence is consciousness, not skills and information, and that consciousness is what we all had before we had to play dumb to conform to some imposed idea of ourselves as "children." When you play dumb long enough you become dumb. This is where women and children have arrived at the close of the patriarchal revolution. My more conscious "children" initiated my liberation from the twilight of my life as an educated dumb woman. I looked all around me and saw nothing but dumb adults and a lot of dumb children and mostly unconscious men who had forgotten their original reasons for making their women and children so dumb. Women's liberation will mean the liberation of children. The end of motherhood (and of course fatherhood) means an end to parent chauvinism and child oppression, and end to private property and authoritative representation. Women already are standing up and saying that being a mother in a ticky-tacky box looking after her possessions is an abnormal unhealthy situation. That we may be the *instruments* of creation, but we have no right to own and dominate our products after we provide the nourishments of the abjectly dependent stage. That no woman can become herself in service to dependents for whom she is the sole source of guidance and well-being. That women like men have become slaves to the fabrication of parental superiority. That parental chauvinism in the first place was an invention of the father. And all the other interrelated reasons for terminating the source unit of large-scale worldwide oppression by class, race, age, and sex: the modern patriarchal nuclear family. As I see it the movement for child-care centers is an important transitional measure on the way back to the large communal families of multiple parents. Such families exist in the hippie commune form and they remain oppressive of women. Possibly the only "liberated" communal families at this time are the lesbian mother households—the total child-care center. A cooperative community of little adults and big children merging identities and responsibilities and exchanging skills and information in an atmosphere of consciousness and mutual respect. The Amazon solution is coming back as one valid kind of social institution. Such an institution constitutes its own legality. Certainly the protection of a larger group should be attractive to any lesbian mother who wants to keep her child and has reason to fear the law. The woman alone or living the nuclear family model with another woman is more vulnerable to the whims of an angry jealous father who has every right to claim custody under his own system by impugning the character of his ex-wife. The larger group is no certain protection, but it a politically conscious community with internal resources for maintaining its integrity and a revolutionary stake in doing so. To women at last acutely aware of belonging to a class under siege and who enjoy sharing all aspects of their lives with other women, such communities make eminent sense.

The More Profound Nationality of their Lesbianism:
Lesbian Society in Paris in the 1920's

Bertha Harris

Now I am 35 and have a penchant for old ladies; but then I was 21 and had a penchant for old ladies.

I was 21 and fresh out of The Woman's College of the University of North Carolina (now mediocred to co-ed and called the University of North Carolina at Greensboro); but then it was a woman's college and called itself one. It was also a hotbed of lesbianism: among the native pop it was called a hotbed of lesbianism.

This rumor, thank god, was true.

I was fresh out of the arms of the hotbed of lesbianism and out of the clutches of the closet-sado ex-marine Dean and on the streets of New York: the summer of 1959. And when I was not at my $55.00 a week job I was hanging out on the corner of Patchin Place—not, under any circumstances, to catch a glimpse of e.e. cummings—but waiting for Djuna Barnes to take her afternoon walk and, with all discretion, follow her—moved the way she moved, turn the way she turned, hold my head like her head. As often as I could (and with discretion) I followed her and, trailing her, received the silent messages about my past I needed and she could give; and never once during our exchange did I encroach upon her lordly solitude to give her my name. The name she made up for me was my real name; and it was that name she used, when, in my fantasy, she would stop and take my hand to thank me for all the flowers I daily stuffed into her mailbox in Patchin Place and then tell me how it was to be a dyke in Paris, in the Twenties.

I believed I should have been born to that world: in my twenties, in the Sixties, I knew I should have been born to that world just as I had known, when I was 15, that I was in reality George Sand: cigar, waistcoat, striped trousers, actresses.

77

It never happened. And I never happened in that world and they are all dead now except for Djuna Barnes. Colette and Gertrude Stein and Alice B. Toklas and Sylvia Beach, who published *Ulysses* out of her bookshop; and Una Troubridge and Radclyffe Hall and Mata Hari and Romaine Brooks and Natalie Clifford Barney—all dead but Djuna Barnes whose books I got to read by prevaricating my way into the New York Public Library rare book room (my phoney ID proclaimed me Dr. Valerie von Trilling, Cambridge: I wore a dumpy tweed skirt, a starched white shirt, black necktie) but whose books are no longer rare, are now being reprinted for sundry and all.

The main trouble with hero worship is that the postman has one hell of a time getting the telephone bill past the scrunched up sweetheart roses.

Back at alma mater Hotbed, we Englit majors had never heard a word of any of them. Our teachers had never heard a word of any of them—or, if they had, had dismissed the word as inconsequential compared to those of the real makers and breakers and shakers of modern literature: those men with the paperback book names. It took more than talent, it was obscurely made plain; it also took balls. Gertrude Stein, they told us, was Hemingway's teacher.

Educational Phase Two, therefore—the education of the lesbian into artist into lesbian into scholar into dyke—was delayed until New York and the Phoenix Bookshop on Cornelia Street where the nice owner urged *Nightwood* on me for seventy-five cents and I met on the upper west side the most elegant of all Firbankian heroes who toured the night streets with me and called out at the gates of Patchin Place, "Watchman, What of the Night?" And he too wished for himself that world where neither of us had happened, playing let's pretend that he was in truth Miss Radclyffe Hall and was wearing pearl earrings like his favorite actress Miss Eva LeGallienne and that I was Eva's lover, Miss Margaret Webster. We roamed the streets making up our histories as we went along and gradually I no longer saw myself as beginning and ending with *The Well of Loneliness*: I was shadowing Djuna Barnes. Colette could be bought. *The Autobiography of Alice B. Toklas* became my book of ancestors. But I was poor and grubby; naive, emotional, sweaty with lowerclass need. I was short and peasantmade—and my ancestors, I learned, as I read my censored history, were rich or nearly rich; sophisticated, cool; longlimbed; and our family bloodline, the common identity among us, would always be nothing more, nothing less, than our common need for the word of consequence: will always be my acknowledgement of these women, despite all material difference between us, as my first ancestors, the women my father stole me from. Like every other dyke with a book in her hand, I know that these are the women our fathers stole us from. Know thy women: know thyself; and the miracle of changeling into hero is accomplished.

They were American and English and French but mostly American but with the father's nationality in effect wiped out by the more profound nationality of their lesbianism. From the turn of the century and into the Twenties, they escaped the American Gothic with huge hunks of papa's fortune stuffed in their pockets—fortunes made for the most part by the usual grinding-the-noses-of-the-poor and fortunes spent by these women solely on themselves and on each other; and they took immense pleasure in the spending. Gradually, as they spent, they wrote and met and talked; and gradually their mythologies and definitions began to emerge. They never, for instance, experienced the guilt that assails many of the nowadays sisters about being richer and better educated and better dressed and better looking than the lesbians on the other side of the tracks. The world, as they saw it, was quite naturally divided into rigid class systems and into gay and straight; and, in their extension of such logic, to be upper class was at its finest to be also gay. Even if she were raised by a washerwoman, as was the case with Romaine Brooks, her lesbianism gave her automatic rank as an aristocrat: to be lesbian was at its finest to be also upper class. In general, all that was heterosexual was "ugliness" and all that was lesbian, "beautiful"; and they spent their time in refined enactment of that which was beautiful and fleeing from that which they knew as ugliness. It took great effort: modern times, they lamented, made little room for that beauty which was ultimate; and rather like my elegant faggot who was yearning in 1960 for their world, they directed their energies towards the recreation of what they wanted to be their ancestry, an age of Sappho delightful with lyric paganism, attic abandonment: a time still uncorrupted by the sickness of the Judeo-Christian ethic.

It was around Natalie Clifford Barney that most of this society revolved, probably because she had the most money and (perhaps as a direct result of the most money) the deepest commitment to the pursuit of the beautiful and the ressurection of attic ecstacy. Her search is crystallized in a volume of verse she had privately printed in 1911 to which she signed herself "une jeune fille de la Societié future." Entitled *Cinq Petits Dialogues Grecs (Antithèses et Parallèles)*, the little book exalts the passions of Lesbos in the manner of Pierre Louys (*Songs of Bilitis*) to whom it is dedicated and reveals to the contemporary reader conscious of such things a talent deformed and for the most part smothered by the necessity to hide behind a gilt-edged romantic depravity:

Soeur de L'Aphrodita, Lesbos, fille d l'oude
Conçue étrangement, plus troublante et
    divine
De rester incomprise . . . isolée androgne
Dans ta perversité savamment inféconde

Venge-toi du mépris de la Laideur immonde
Qui se Nomme Vertu, que sa lourde racine
Porte le fruit pesant, laissant ma voix câline
Dire les autres mouers de tout un autre
    monde.

Lesbos, belle Lesbos, de tes levres blémis
Réveille la beauté de tes Amours célèbres
Leur volupté défunte et leur gloire outragée

Pour toi je veux chanter, amante des amies,
Ecoute ma chanson du lit bleu de l'Egée
Et souris-moi, Sapho, du fond de tes
    ténèbres.
        ("Sonnet")

On her green lawn at Neiully, in the drawing room of her Renaissance house, the others came to talk, dance, drink lemonade and eat cake (Miss Barney despised alcohol) and to reweave the threads of sexual intrigue. From all accounts, she was "Amazonian" in appearance; and, every morning, dressed all in white, rode her horse through the Bois. Another American escapee, Romaine Brooks, was her friend and lover from 1915 until 1970—they died within two years of each other—and among Brooks' paintings of women, which only recently have begun to receive some appropriate attention, the portrait of Natalie Barney is remarkable for its intimacy of expression, its softness of portrayal; and it was only for Natalie Barney's poetry readings that Romaine Brooks would leave her work.

In her outrageous lesbian comedy, *Almanack for Ladies*, Djuna Barnes focusses on Natalie Barney and her drawing room and her bedroom to portray the complexities of the social and sexual games of her little world. Privately printed in 1928 and "anonymously" presented by "A Lady of Fashion," the little book not only satirized such famous figures of the inner circle as Radclyffe Hall and Una Troubridge ("Lady Buck-and-Balk and Tilly-Tweed-in-Blood") it is also in its way and for its time, a document of lesbian revolution. Baroque, fanciful and precious on the one hand and passionately serious on the other, it is a mirror image of the psychology of Natalie Barney's intensely exclusive milieu. Lesbians are made in Heaven, Djuna Barnes seems to say; and they are the children of angels: "This is the part about Heaven that has never been told . . . . there was heard under the Dome of Heaven a great Crowing, and from the Midst, an Egg, as incredible as a thing forgotten, fell to Earth, and striking, split and hatched, and from out of it stepped one saying 'Pardon me, I must be going!' And this was the first Woman born with a Difference. After this the Angels parted, and the Face of each was the Mother look. Why was that?" Like the work of Romaine Brooks, this book has only recently been drawn out of rare book room obscurity and reissued by Harper and Row.

Unfortunately, Natalie Barney felt it necessary to admit men as well as lesbians into her house. For one of her scope, it is possible that there were simply not enough free women of sufficient talent and intellect around at the time to fulfill her grand design. For whatever reasons, such notables as Gide and Pound were permitted to pay their homage in person (although one wonders if it were in tribute to her poetry or in payment for the richness of her salon and/or patronage); and one infamous day, Pound gained the favor of presenting to her the ostentatiously super-Yank, William Carlos Williams. Williams, too, in his *Autobiography*, praises her; but true to his culture, which associates super-Art with super-Prick, he ends his brief account of his visit with an anecdote designed to obliterate the impression he had given of a charming and cultured woman: ". . . some member of the Chamber of Deputies, a big, red-faced guy who had turned up there after a routine social acceptance . . . . saw women about him, dancing gaily together on all sides. Thereupon he undid his pants buttons, took out his tool and, shaking it right and left, yelled out in a rage, 'Have you never seen one of these?' " It is a scene reminiscent of the one in Hemingway's *A Movable Feast* in which the Great Amerikan Author-Hero seeks to cast Gertrude Stein (from whom he learned all he ever knew about the use of the English language) into outer darkness by describing his own shriveling shock and disgust upon overhearing an intimate exchange between her and Alice. But in my infuriated fantasies about the moment in Natalie Barney's salon, I like to imagine the part that might never have happened; or, if it did, that Mr. Williams chose to omit: that, at a nod from Miss Barney, the women stopped dancing, snatched up the silly Chamber of Deputies fucker by his exposed "tool" and threw him out the window. Even this is a mild response compared to the great precedent set by the Maenads when they discovered Pentheus spying on their rites which involved—at the very least—some dancing: with his own mother leading the pack, they tore the fellow's head off.

Small wonder that all things Greek were a constant source of inspiration for Miss Barney's set. Although Sappho, of course, was their ideal and it was her work and life-style they sought to emulate (according to their own rather voluptuous interpretations of both), they would inevitably have also known of the fierce and magic women of Greek tragedy and myth—women who would kill their own children to revenge themselves on a man; women who could change themselves into trees to protect themselves from rape.

Armed with money and distinguished connections, such women as Natalie Barney could retreat into a refurbished sense of the past, could actualize their fantasies of freedom, could act out, in privacy, the lesbian virtues. Like Gertrude Stein, but set on a different course of less work and more play, Natalie Barney outdid even the French in the great tradition of the intellectual salon. Pierre Louÿs chanted his *Chansons de Bilitis* to her guests; Colette, as a young woman and even then rising to fame on her own name as the author of the Claudine novels, took part in elaborate tableaux staged in the garden. In *My*

Apprenticeships and Music-Hall Sidelights, Colette recounts her appearance in Louys' "Dialogue au soleil couchant," playing with the American, Miss Eva Palmer who, with an abundance of red hair and clothed in "more or less" a Greek tunic, created a dazzling picture with Colette who was playing Daphnis in "crepe de Chine, a pair of Roman Buskins and a wreath in the Tahiti style." But their theatrical triumph, marked by Louys' praise ("I have experienced one of the greatest emotions of my life") was short-lived. Immediately following Colette's and Eve Palmer's act, a naked woman on a white horse rode out of the bushes. She was a new dancer making her name in the studio and drawingroom cliques, Mata Hari, remembered now only for "female" wartime intrigue. Emma Calve, another friend of the sisterhood, sponsored Colette's appearance at one of her own afternoons. Colette, in the same account of this era of her long life, tells of how she danced "supported by a little group of colored attendants and musicians and framed in the pillars of a vast, white hall . . . snake-like and enigmatic . . . ." Of the conclusion of the dance, when she was finally naked entire, Colette writes that she carried "the male—and a good proportion of the female—spectators to the extreme limit of decent attention."

Such was the quality of lesbian entertainment in the days of our ancestors. But Colette created sensations also on the public stage, sensations which have found political fulfillment only in our time during such events as Jill Johnston's famous zap on Mailer & Co. at Town Hall. On January 3, 1907, Colette, with her lover the Marquise de Belboeuf, created the Scandale du Moulin-Rouge. At the climax of their performance in a pantomime ("Reve d'Egypte") there was a kiss between the two women of such explicitness that it brought not only the roof of the theatre down but also an injunction from the police against further performance.

Such events in Colette's life have been largely ignored outside homosexual literature or have been reduced to footnotes and asides by those who have sought to reduce this highly complex artist to merely the heterosexual aspects of her personality. That she found her greatest happiness in the company of her adored mother, Sido; that she spent more time divorced than married, that she was as precise in depicting her erotic relationships with women as she was in writing of her life with men and that her writing which evokes the sensual nature of women—their bodies, scents, clothing—is the best of its kind, seems to indicate that she was something more than the determinedly straight woman she reformed herself into in her later life.

Only the year before the "Scandale" with the Marquise, Colette had achieved a divorce from the nasty little "Willy," who had made a nice reputation for himself by publishing her work under his own name, and had gone off to live with the Marquise who was known to intimates as Missy.

On Capri, which had a long tradition of indulgence for moneyed deviants on holiday from the rigors of Paris, the pair lived out their style openly together and were members of the group around Natalie Barney and her then-lover, Renee Vivien, who was the most flamboyant and ultimately the most victimized of the women the group contained. Roger Peyrefitte, in his novel, *L'Exile de Capri*, writes that Colette wore "bracelets engraved 'I belong to Missy' " while the Marquise "dressed in a tuxedo, would reminisce, between two puffs on her cigar, about 'the great Morny, my father.' " High drag and its concommittant role-playing/plying abounded. But it is also during this same period that Colette wrote the rhapsodic "Night without Sleep" which opens:

> In our house there is only one bed, too big for you, a little narrow for us both. It is chaste, white, completely exposed; no drapery veils its honest candor in the light of day. People who come to see us survey it calmly and do not tactfully look aside, for it is marked, in the middle, with but one soft valley, like the bed of a young girl who sleeps alone.
>
> They do not know, those who enter here, that every night the weight of our two united bodies hollows out a little more, beneath its voluptuous winding sheet . . . .

A long way from the "Lesbians Ignite" sign on the living room wall but, perhaps, its necessary precedent.

In a letter to Leon Hamel, at about the same time, Colette allows us further evidence with which to reconstruct the world of her youth: "We heard . . . that . . . the Baroness Van Zuylen lorded it in a box, wearing white tie and tails—and a mustache! The Baroness Ricoy accompanied her, likewise in tails and looking quite emaciated beside that elephantine monster. They were recognized and were pestered . . . although the Baroness Van Zuylen responded to the intruders with broadsides of very masculine oaths."

From Paris to Capri, the little world floated back and forth on its substantial bank accounts, intent on pleasure, intent on disguising serious work, serious anger, with masks of frivolity; cushioning rejection with luxury—all in the manner of the last-of-the-line aristocrat: life itself was a vulgarity; passion was honed to its keenest cutting edge.

Even through its vision of camp, it is possible to detect much of the reality of the life in Compton Mackenzie's novel, *Extraordinary Women*: Grouped around the Bay of Naples, a society of continental women pass their days and nights in what amounts to the giving of parties, the going to parties, the seduction of the sweetest and the newest, engagement in sexual warfare. Their greatest fear is to be caught out in an excess of emotion or to be confronted with the crudities of the workaday (straight) world. Monocled, tuxedoed butches pursue their seductive opposites; and, beyond a knowledge of the requisite Greek, the tango, and the ability to make love in French, there is seldom a woman the whole book long who is allowed to be wise, gracious, learned. The novel parodys them parodying themselves. Radclyffe Hall, being a woman instead of a Compton Mackenzie, is able, even in the tiresome martyrdom of her prose, to let one of them shine: *The Well of Loneliness* character, Valerie—sophisticated, kind, incipiently revolutionary—is probably based on Natalie Clifford Barney. But that all of them knew their stuff and that some of them found the energy to write the stuff of their experience at least as well as most of their overdocumented straight contemporaries, is in none of them more conclusively proved than in the life and work of Renee Vivien.

She was born Pauline Tarn, daughter of a British father and American mother and was dead of tuberculosis and self-induced starvation and drugs and drink and sealed windows by the age of 32. The life both created and killed what little breathing and working she could muster. But before she died she wrote some of the most outspoken poetry concerning lesbian passion since Sappho—work which has been described by Colette as being of "unequal strength, force, merit, unequal as the human breath, as the pulsations of human suffering." She was the contemporary of Baudelaire; her poetry rises

85

frequently from the same sources; but while the man's name is as much a household word in literary circles as a detergent's is in daytime tv, the woman's is inaudible. With her young lover, Natalie Barney, she sought to recreate the world of women Sappho had made at Mytilene. Arriving (literally) at the island of Lesbos, the women rented two villas joined by an orchard and did their best to give new life to the old rites—and, very shortly defeated by the modern Christian world, were back in Paris.

Renee Vivien's short life—and her oppression as worker, woman and lesbian—can best be summarized in two pieces of writing. Her epitaph on her tomb at Pass reads:

> Here lies my enraptured heart
> At peace, sleeping
> Since, for the love of death,
> It has pardoned the crime which is life.

And in a *Souvenir* by Colette: ". . . Renee wandered, not so much clad as veiled in black or purple, almost invisible in the scented darkness of the immense rooms barricaded with leaded windows, the air heavy with curtains and incense. Three or four times I caught her curled up in the corner of a divan, scribbling with a pencil . . . . On these occasions she always sprang up guiltily, excusing herself, murmuring, 'It's nothing, I've finished now . . .'"

It is fruitless to speculate on the amount and quality of the work the woman could have produced had her life and sexuality, as a woman, as a lesbian, not been suffocated by a vicious moral code which caused in her—as in millions of other women—the need to enact as quickly as possible the death which a sexist world insisted it must have in sacrifice.

When a woman, especially a lesbian woman, attempts suicide, she is in reality being murdered. What we, the heirs of the victim, have left from Renee Vivien's long suicide, are a few passionate lyrics. I have been told that her family has ensured that nothing more of her work will be released until the year 2,000. She wrote to Natalie Barney:

> I fear the pearly shimmer
> of your tender breasts, trembling
> I touch your Godgiven body
> I fear the delights of your mouth.

Catholicism was one of the major weapons used in the

psychological destruction of these women. Seduced by the secretiveness of ritual, by the incense, color and most particularly by the nature of its death-wishing drama, most of these women succumbed to its invidiousness at some point in their lives, being offered a clear identification of their own suffering with that of the crucified christ's—and, at the same time, an opportunity to increase their pain (through the channels offered by the religion) to meet the demands of the phallic world for more bloodletting.

In *The Life and Death of Radclyffe Hall*, Lady Una Troubridge reflects this heterosexist-induced masochism in its extremity. With ghastly eagerness, she spends much of her effort in this biography of her lover in detailing the "spiritual" life of our ancestral dykes. She and her "John" cherished, she writes, a splinter of the "true cross" and when they had to travel to unsuitable places, a buddy cherished it for them. Working up to her description of Radclyffe Hall's death, she first tells us of the "mystical" experience which gave her comfort after the death of her beloved: ". . . John and I celebrated my birthday at Lucca, together with thirty-five friends from Florence who had eagerly accepted our invitation. We ourselves arrived overnight, with Sandra Tealdi, May Massola, Eliza Imperiali and Fonfi Piccone, all of them bound to us by ties of affection, all of them united to us in faith and anxious to join us in receiving Holy Communion at the shrine on the morning of the pilgrimage. At noon . . . we all made our way to San Martino to see the most wonderful Face in the world . . . . for only at Lucca perhaps in all the world can one truly understand why, when He spoke to men, they put down their nets and followed Him . . . . I did not know, when I adored that splendour, that the day was not very far ahead when He would speak to me through utter bereavement and demand that I should tread the way of loneliness; but He knew it and perhaps it was for that reason that He gave me the memory of His Holy Face."

It is, more than likely, this mania for *mea culpa* conditioned in them from the beginnings of their sexuality, that is even more revolting than their elitism, their decadence, their snobbery, to the revolutionary dykedom of today. Between Sappho and Gertrude Stein, however, these women represent practically the only available expressions of lesbian culture we have in the modern western world:

87

and, if women as a whole have scant history of themselves, lesbians are even more bereft of such bridges on which they can make their transitions from past to future. Male homosexual literature, from Plato to Shakespeare to Genet, because it is male and emerges from phallic privilege, has been accorded esteem, respect, honor to the written word; but there is no male literature that is not intrinsically homosexual—women being in most instances, however, a more readily convenient vessal for assault than the revered ass-hole of another man: and women becoming in male literature simply a convenient symbol of ass-hole, a means of fucking the god through the medium of the slave. There is no literature that is not based on the pervasive sexuality of its time; and as that which is male disappears (sinks slowly in the west) and as the originally all-female world reasserts itself by making love to itself, the primary gesture toward the making at last of a decent literature out of the experience of a decent world might simply be a woman like myself following a woman like Djuna Barnes, and all she might represent, down a single street on a particular afternoon.

The Comingest Womanifesto

Jill Johnston

first or second off i'm into thinking weird all in these difference places in fact in as many places as we are women and so i ask myself when i meet this one or that one i ask where is them politically sexually & where is one in relation to this one or me or where am i now sexually politically since i'm not the me i was yesterday or last year and where are we going or am i already ahead of myself or behind and is somebody else slightly behind or ahead of that and if not then what or what anything i mean how should we behave and where should we think or what are we permitted to assume much less concerning anybody else their total life their total past who are they who am i who am i to them to become if anything & so on like is the one i'm talking to about to sleep with a woman for the first time in which case would i cause her not to if i accused her of oppressing me by being the kind of a woman who sleeps with the man and if she does anyway will she then be terrified to think she might be thought a lesbian and if so should we condemn her for thinking what we were all brought up all these centuries to actually think altho we now think we're so smart just because a few of us now know that it not only isn't bad it's great in fact it's the best and that that when you ponder it makes us the Ultimate Feminists etc. i mean we think we're really hot shit and we are and so what is that gonna do for us when so many women are still so scared the question is do we want more of us or do we want to just go around saying what hot shit we are and how you straight women are lousing us up just to make sure they'll go on doing it and if so how long would it take before the women called lesbians reemerge as a special interest group and how long after that before you can't say the word lesbian at all any more as if there *is* such a thing as a lesbian the boggler being the more i say it the more i feel it doesn't exist since so

many women now actually are lesbians and you wouldn't hear
anybody anymore say well huff huff this woman must be a lesbian
because she hated her father and her mother was a bitch or whatever
they say along those lines or she got to be a lesbian harumph because
she had a terrible first sexual experience with a man and all that you
wouldn't hear that except in these clinical psychiatric journals anyway
even tho from this new point of view there may be no such thing as a
lesbian any more and besides which we know now that all lesbians are
women i have to go on saying it to make sure anybody knows i'm
defining myself politically as a woman committed woman and the
word feminist to me doesn't totally convey that idea since so many
feminists advocate a change in our situation in relation to the man
rather than the devotion of our energies to our own kind to women i
have to ask does this make us enemies when we are all potentially
dedicated to ourselves and when we believe in feminist issues per se
i.e., abortion reform and when we are in a sense each of us all the
women we ever were including straight possibly just yesterday or last
year or the last time i slept with a man two years ago or four years
before that in a tenement on houston street with two kids still
thinking i was straight and i was even tho i was in love with a woman i
still am that woman i am all the women i ever was which is all the
women of the world in transition i become more completely a lesbian
or woman commited woman as the centuries pass and more of me
becomes me or the me i think it's such hot shit to be which it is by
which i mean a woman the more i sleep with myself and eat myself
and write myself and breathe myself the more woman i become i
become the woman myself i am who i sleep with it doesn't mean
you're not a lesbian if you never slept with a woman before if you
consider the person you sleep with the most is yourself and that's you
a woman from this point of view we all are lesbians right from the
start altho what we are and what we think or say we are can be
altogether different things it doesn't matter even by the sights of
advanced ideology you can't demand that people be where they're not
yet ready to be even if you say all persuasive and important listen a
woman committed to herself meaning a woman as combined image of
mother daughter and sister was is absolutely at odds with society
which has been in the modern western world organized around the

principle of heterosexuality which in effect means the prime commitment of woman to man who is committed to himself or saying it another way if you say what i really mean when i say you're oppressing me when you sleep with the man is that you're giving something so vital to the man is the same as withholding it from me your daughter your sister or how in effect you go to bed with my brother by paying him more attention you deprive me in proportion as you do so is all very good logic possibly especially when we can say furthermore look you who have for centuries given your best services to your sons what in the end have the sons done for us if not to persuade us or coerce us to serve more sons okay and go on and say and look around you do you see any lesbians becoming straight and so on no matter what we say however i'm convinced we can't very well demand what anybody isn't ready to give who may in fact be ready to change tomorrow or next year who may know a lot more in advance of her current opportunities or her present practical situation or emotional readiness or who may be putting her life in order to make big changes we don't know about anyway who probably won't be significantly impressed by anything so much as the example of our own togetherness all of which doesn't alter it's true the social fact that the very women we wait for continue to hurt us by damning us or ignoring us or hating us or tolerating us or condescending us for loving ourselves or oppressing us by objectifying us as potential Lesbian Experiences or projecting onto us the sexism and puritanism and chauvinism of their own expectations of all they've known in relation to the man we won't stop them from doing this by accusing them of it or by objectifying them in turn by say making any woman a princess or an all purpose mommie or even necessarily by carrying on about how when you saw me at that party and said so you have breasts what you meant was so you're a woman after all like a guy saying to a faggot in a locker room you really do have balls as though a lesbian or woman committed women is less than a woman or somehow a male for liking other women the way males do supposedly and thus being less a woman not being a woman in the sisterhood of man pandering females or when you say oh i happen to love a woman now but i could as well have a relationship with a man if he were the right sort of person as tho we were not all *persons* before the *feminists* taught us we were women in the sense of being a political class in which case what you're really saying is if the right sort of *man* came along or when you say if all else fails we'll try loving our sisters as if your sister was a last resort and even if you do think you mean just sex i translate it to mean loving your sisters which means sex and *every*thing i still know the truth is demonstrable only by example and the only way to proceed historically is to respect personal places places even we feel are detaining us or delaying us or detering us we respect them nevertheless for being the places any woman is capable of being the way we respect a wasp for being a wasp we don't condemn a wasp for being the type of animal who would sting us if she could i don't want to pursue the example the example that concerns me here is the assertion of our own logic and model in this way enough women by a few centuries time will become the hot shit we think we are to make a viable amazon nation or tribe or tribes of women capable of sustaining themselves independently of the male specious we have to remind ourselves that in 1972 in amerika we are a fugitive band who can't afford to isolate ourselves from the woman in the middle who in any case remains a potentially total ally or the woman we are gradually becoming as we become more of ourselves as we leave more of our straight selves of ourselves behind ourselves we gradually become ourselves all the women we ever were we are ourselves still the woman in the middle it doesn't make any sense to be our own enemy and if we don't see common cause with feminists feminists are not likely to see it with us either especially when it's so easy to find reason by offense to say we'll have nothing to do with you when it's still so scary to proclaim the legitimacy of an identity so recently criminal or sick or sinful we must therefore as i see it take all the chances and risk being the ones to continue being hurt and insulted by exposing our thought as the logic of the feminist/lesbian position and exposing our selves as the models of the revolution by realizing we are each and all all the women of the world in transition and not placing ourselves thus above and beyond or ahead but directly in the center as the moving force of our collective conscience.

Resolution of Lesbians International*

Resolution of Lesbians International in its western hemispherical conference of an estimated 70,000 lesbians at the Lavender Whale Inn, Round Grove, Missouri:

Lesbians International came out in favor of feminist rights.

Whereas, because she defines herself in relation to men, the straight feminist is considered unnatural, incomplete, not quite a woman—as though the essence of womanhood were to be identified with women; and

Whereas, feminists were never excluded from Lesbians International, but we have been evasive or apologetic about their presence within the organization. Afraid of encouraging public (i.c. male) support, we have often treated feminists as the step-sisters of the movement, allowed them to work with us, but then expected them to hide in the upstairs closet when the company comes. Asking women to disguise their identities so that they will not "embarrass" the group is an intolerable form of oppression, like asking white women to join us in black face. Lesbians International must reassess the priorities that sacrifice principles to "image."

Whereas, we are affected by society's prejudices against the heterosexual woman whether we acknowledge it or not: as lesbians we are all subject to straight-baiting by opponents who use the tactic of labeling us the worst thing they can think of, "heterosexual," in order to divide and discredit the movement and bring women to heel. Even within Lesbians International this tactic has been employed by some members who insist that feminists are a special interest group whose primary concern is men. Lesbians International is inevitably weakened by these attempts to undermine the spirit and efforts of its members; we can no longer afford to ignore the problem.

Therefore, be it resolved: That Lesbians International recognizes feminism as a lesbian issue.

*This piece is a very slight modification—a turn-about—of a resolution of the National Organization for Women (N.O.W.) which "recognized lesbianism as a feminist issue."

Books from Times Change Press

JANUARY THAW: People at Blue Mt. Ranch Write About Living Together in the Mountains. Writing about relationships, work, parents, children, healing and celebration, these rural communards describe feeling their way toward a life that makes sense and feels good, in which people are more in harmony with themselves, each other, the earth and the universe. *Illustrated; 160 pp; $3.25. Cloth, $8.50.*

THE EARLY HOMOSEXUAL RIGHTS MOVEMENT (1864-1935)—John Lauritsen and David Thorstad. The gay movement, like the women's movement, has an early history, which, beginning in 1864, advanced the cause of gay rights until the 1930s when Stalinist and Nazi repression obliterated virtually all traces of it. The authors uncover this history, highlighting interesting people and events. *Illustrated; 96 pp; $2.25. Cloth, $6.95.*

MOMMA: A Start on All the Untold Stories—Alta. This is Alta's intensely personal story of her life with her two young daughters, and her struggle to be a writer. She tells of her efforts toward self-fulfillment and her battle against feelings of guilt—a story many readers will recognize as their own. *Illustrated; 80 pp; $2.00. Cloth, $6.50.*

AMAZON EXPEDITION: A Lesbianfeminist Anthology—Edited by Phyllis Birkby, Bertha Harris, Jill Johnston, Esther Newton and Jane O'Wyatt. When lesbians within the gay liberation movement synthesized gay politics with feminism, they started a separate political/cultural development which thousands of women began to identify with. This is what this anthology is about. Culture, herstory, politics, celebration. Lesbianfeminism—one concept: the new womanity. *Illustrated; 96 pp; $2.25. Cloth, $6.50.*

LISTEN TO THE MOCKING BIRD: Satiric Songs To Tunes You Know—Tuli Kupferberg. Radical songs can't make the new world, but they can help. And they can help you endure this one. Especially if they're humorous. Over 50 songs to delight and thrill you and yes make you laugh. *Illustrated; 64 pp; $1.50.*

THIS WOMAN: Poetry of Love and Change—Barbara O'Mary. This journal tells of a year of intense change—involving Barbara's lovers male and female, her daughters, her job, her politics, her fears, her visions. Simple, intimate and honest poetry which we identify with immediately, as it clarifies our own experience. *Illustrated; 64 pp; $1.50.*

LESSONS FROM THE DAMNED: Class Struggle in the Black Community—By The Damned. This book describes the awareness of oppression as black people, as workers and poor people under capitalism, and as women and young people oppressed by men and the family. It may be the first time that poor and petit-bourgeois black people have told their own story. *Illustrated; 160 pp; $2.75. Cloth, $7.95.*

SOME PICTURES FROM MY LIFE: A Diary—Marcia Salo Rizzi. Marcia has selected entries from her diary and combined them with her emotionally powerful ink-brush drawings—one woman's experience reflecting pictures from the lives of all women. *Illustrated; 64 pp; $1.35.*

GREAT GAY IN THE MORNING!: One Group's Approach to Communal Living and Sexual Politics—The 25 to 6 Baking & Trucking Society. These are personal accounts of seven gay men and two lesbians writing about their experiences in over three years of communal living, gay consciousness-raising, and political involvement. *Illustrated; 96 pp; $2.25. Cloth, $4.95.*

BEGIN AT START: Some Thoughts on Personal Liberation and World Change—Su Negrin. A Times Change Press editor writes about her experiences in various liberation movements (mysticism, free school, commune, new left, feminist and gay) and talks about how they're all coming together in a new way—transforming individuals and approaching a utopia more awesome than we have ever dreamed of. *Illustrated; 176 pp; $2.75. Cloth, $6.95.*

YOUTH LIBERATION: News, Politics and Survival Information—Youth Liberation of Ann Arbor. The authors write about the oppression of being young in an adult chauvinist society—imprisonment in families and schools, economic dependence, denial of legal rights—and they describe the growing activity toward world-wide youth liberation. *Illustrated; 64 pp; $1.75.*

FREE OURSELVES: Forgotten Goals of the Revolution—Arthur Aron; Illustrations by Elaine N. Blesi. In our movement for social change, we have in many ways, lost touch with our humanistic values. Art believes that to realize our values we must *live* them—now—by changing ourselves and creating a giant personal/social/cultural alternative. *Illustrated; 64 pp; $1.35.*

WOODHULL AND CLAFLIN'S WEEKLY: The Lives and Writings of Victoria Woodhull and Tennessee Claflin—Arlene Kisner, Editor/Biographer. Throughout their notorious careers, Victoria and Tennie were involved in the radical developments of their time—socialism, mysticism, women's rights. These selections from their (in)famous newsmagazine (1870-1876) are interspersed with Arlene's detailed biographical sketches. *Illustrated; 64 pp; $1.35.*

UNBECOMING MEN: A Men's Consciousness-Raising Group Writes on Oppression and Themselves. This book reflects the struggles of a group of men who've come together because of their increasingly unavoidable awareness of sexism—how it operates against the people they most care for and ultimately, how it eats away at their own humanity. *Illustrated; 64 pp; $1.75.*

GENERATIONS OF DENIAL: 75 Short Biographies of Women in History—Kathryn Taylor. These women were whole people under the worst of circumstances, worse still for those who, in addition to being female, were gay. These biographies are a pioneering collection with which to supplement history books and women's pride. *Illustrated; 64 pp; $1.35.*

BURN THIS AND MEMORIZE YOURSELF: Poems for Women—Alta; Photographs by Ellen Shumsky. An unusual pamphlet of plain-talking poems, set against a background of photographs, showing women in many of the new ways they are beginning to be together—self-sufficient, intimate, loving, self-defined. *Illustrated; 16 pp; 50¢.*

FREE SPACE: A Perspective on the Small Group in Women's Liberation—Pamela Allen. *Free Space* is a good handbook for people wondering how to begin or restructure a consciousness-raising group. Developed by feminists, the small group is now being used by many people as a way of relating to different needs. *Illustrated; 64 pp; $1.75.*

ECOLOGY AND REVOLUTIONARY THOUGHT—Murray Bookchin. This book widens the scope of the ecological problem by asserting that people's domination over nature is rooted in our domination over each other. Murray takes into account the social/political crises that are inseparable from our environmental one. *Illustrated; 64 pp; $1.25.*

THE TRAFFIC IN WOMEN and Other Essays on Feminism—Emma Goldman; with a biography by Alix Kates Shulman. Emma Goldman was a dynamic anarchist and so her feminism differed markedly from her suffrage-oriented contemporaries. Today the split between liberal and radical approaches to women's liberation are still not resolved. So these essays have an uncanny relevancy to problems now being dealt with. *Illustrated; 64 pp; $1.35.*

Times Change Press also produces good quality, inexpensive
POSTERS
They are illustrated in our *free catalog*
which you can get by writing to the address below.

TO ORDER ANY OF THE ABOVE,

SEND CASH, CHECK OR MONEY ORDER
(including 35¢ postage & handling per order)

TO: TIMES CHANGE PRESS
62 W. 14th St.
New York, N. Y. 10011
